Tobacco Plant Varieties
for
Home Growers

by
Robert C.A. Goff

Dreamsplice
Christiansburg, Virginia

2   *Robert C.A. Goff*

Tobacco Plant Varieties for Home Growers

Copyright © 2022 by Dreamsplice
First edition: September 2022

This work is licensed under the Creative Commons Attribution-ShareAlike 4.0 International License. To view a copy of this license, visit http://creativecommons.org/licenses/by/4.0/ or send a letter to Creative Commons, PO Box 1866, Mountain View, CA 94042, USA.

You may distribute it and/or modify it under the terms of the Creative Commons Attribution License (http://creativecommons.org/licenses/by/4.0/), version 4.0 or later.

Image credits:
    NWT: Northwood Seeds
    ARS-GRIN: USDA Agricultural Research Service, Germplasm Resource Information Network
    RCAG: the author
    Others as noted. Any credit preceded by "@" indicates a user name on the Fair Trade Tobacco Forum (fairtradetobacco.com).

ISBN: 979-8-9867728-0-6
Library of Congress Control Number: 2022915049

Dreamsplice
3462 Dairy Road
Christiansburg, VA 24073

www.dreamsplice.com

Contents

Acknowledgments   **15**

Introduction   **17**

   Varieties by Use Class (see Index for alphabetical list)

FLUE-CURED

African Red	**19**
Awa	**20**
Bamboo Shoot	**21**
Banana Leaf	**22**
Big Gem	**23**
Bonanza	**24**
Brown & Williams Low Nicotine	**25**
Bucak	**26**
401 Cherry Red	**27**
Coker 213	**28**
Coker 371-Gold	**29**
Costello Negro	**30**
Crimean	**31**
Delgold	**32**
Dixie Bright 27	**33**
Frog Eye Orinoco	**34**
Gold Dollar	**35**
Gold Leaf	**36**
Gold Leaf Orinoco	**37**
Golden Harvest	**38**
Golden Wilt	**39**
Goyano	**40**
Helena	**41**
Hickory Pryor	**42**

Jaffna	**43**
Lemon Bright	**44**
Lizard Tail Orinoco	**45**
NC 82	**46**
Ostrolist	**47**
Oxford 207	**48**
Paris Wrapper	**49**
Polish	**50**
Reams 158	**51**
Silk Leaf	**52**
Southern Beauty	**53**
Stolak 17	**54**
Ternopolski 7	**55**
Ternopolski 14	**56**
Thailand	**57**
Virginia 15	**58**
Virginia 24	**59**
Virginia 116	**60**
Virginia 647	**61**
Virginia Bright Leaf	**62**
Virginia Gold	**63**
Vesta 64	**64**
White Gold	**65**
White Mammoth	**66**
White Stem Orinoco	**67**
Yellow Gold	**68**
Yellow Leaf	**69**
Yellow Orinoco	**70**
Yellow Pryor	**71**

BURLEY	
Baldío Vera	**72**
Burley 9	**73**
Burley 21	**74**
Burley 64	**75**
Chillard's White Angel Leaf	**76**
Golden Burley	**77**
Green Brior	**78**
Harrow Velvet	**79**
Kelly Burley	**80**
KY 15	**81**
KY 17	**82**
KY 190	**83**
KY 8635	**84**
LI Burley 21	**85**
Moldovan 456	**86**
Monte Calme Yellow (Jaune)	**87**
NB-11	**88**
Sobolchskii	**89**
Sobolchskii 33	**90**
Sobolchskii 193	**91**
Spectrum	**92**
Symbol 4	**93**
TN 86	**94**
TN 86 LC	**95**
TN 90	**96**
TN 90 LC	**97**

Virginia 509	**98**
Yellow Twist Bud	**99**
CIGAR (Wrapper, Binder, Filler)	
Ahus	**100**
Amarello Rio Grande	**101**
Amarillo Parado	**102**
Besuki H382 (Ambulu)	**103**
Besuki H382 (Kesilir)	**104**
Besuki (Java)	**105**
Brasil Dunkel	**106**
Colombian Garcia	**107**
Comstock Spanish	**108**
Connecticut 49	**109**
Connecticut Broadleaf	**110**
Connecticut Shade	**111**
Coroja (Cuba)	**112**
Corojo (Honduras)	**113**
Corojo 99 (Cuba)	**114**
Criollo (Cuba)	**115**
Criollo 98	**116**
Diamantina	**117**
Dixie Shade	**118**
Florida 17	**119**
Florida Sumatra	**120**
Galickii	**121**
Glessnor	**122**
Habano 2000	**123**

Hacienda del Cura	**124**
Havana 142	**125**
Havana 263	**126**
Havana 322	**127**
Havana 38	**128**
Havana 608	**129**
Havana K2	**130**
Havana K2-24	**131**
Havana Z992	**132**
Jalapa	**133**
Jamaica Wrapper	**134**
Kanburi	**135**
L'Assomption 201	**136**
Lancaster Seed Leaf	**137**
Little Dutch	**138**
Long Red	**139**
Machu Picchu Havana	**140**
Magnolia	**141**
Manila Wrapper	**142**
Matsukawa	**143**
Matsukawa Kanto 201	**144**
Metacomet	**145**
Mont-Calme Brun	**146**
Moonlight	**147**
Nacional	**148**
Native 10 (Bolivia)	**149**
No. 3666 Deli	**150**
Nostrano del Brenta	**151**
Ohio Dutch	**152**

Olor (Dominican Republic)	**153**
Pennsylvania Red	**154**
Pergeu	**155**
Piloto Cubano (Puerto Rico)	**156**
Piloto Cubano PR Broad	**157**
Punta De Lanza	**158**
Red Rose	**159**
San Andrés	**160**
Suifu	**161**
Swarr-Hibshman	**162**
Timor	**163**
Uruguay	**164**
Vallejano	**165**
Vuelta Abajo	**166**
Wisconsin 901	**167**
Wisconsin Seedleaf	**168**
Zimmer Spanish	**169**

DARK

Adonis	**170**
Ainaro	**171**
Bolivian Criollo Black	**172**
Goose Creek Red	**173**
Greenwood	**174**
India Black	**175**
Liquiça	**176**
Little Yellow	**177**
Madole	**178**
One Sucker	**179**

Rot Front	**180**
Shirey	**181**
Small Stalk Black Mammoth	**182**
Staghorn	**183**
Szamosi Dark	**184**
Tabaco Negro (Spain)	**185**
VA 355	**186**
Viqueque	**187**
Walker's Broadleaf	**188**

MARYLAND

Catterton	**189**
Keller	**190**
MD A30	**191**
MD 201	**192**
MD 609	**193**
Pennbel 69	**194**
Thompson	**195**

ORIENTAL

Adiyaman	**196**
Alma Ata 315	**197**
American 3	**198**
American 14	**199**
American 26	**200**
American 63	**201**
American 572	**202**
Anatolian	**203**
Bafra	**204**

Bahia	**205**
Baiano	**206**
Balikesir	**207**
Basma	**208**
Bursa	**209**
Canik	**210**
Çelikhan	**211**
Citir	**212**
Djebel 174	**213**
Dukat Crimean	**214**
Düzce	**215**
Ege	**216**
Harmanli	**217**
Harmanliiska Basma 163	**218**
Herzegovina Flor	**219**
Incekara	**220**
Izmir-Karabaglar	**221**
Izmir Ozbas	**222**
Izmir (Lebanon)	**223**
Japan 8	**224**
Krumovgrad 58	**225**
Kumanovo	**226**
Lattaquie 92	**227**
Meechurinski	**228**
Mutki	**229**
Native 9 (Bolivia)	**230**
Nevrokop 5	**231**
Prancak N-1	**232**
Prilep 66-9/7	**233**
Prilep 79-94	**234**

Rejina	**235**
Samsun	**236**
Samsun Maden	**237**
Shirazi	**238**
Simox	**239**
Smyrna 9	**240**
Sultansko	**241**
Tasova	**242**
Tekkekoy	**243**
Tekne	**244**
Trabzon	**245**
Turkish 1	**246**
Turkish 2	**247**
Variegata Samsun	**248**
Vavilov	**249**
White Flower (Cuzco)	**250**
Xanthi-Yaka 18A	**251**
Xanthy	**252**
Yayladag	**253**
Yenidje	**254**
ORNAMENTAL	
Affinis	**255**
Jasmine	**256**
Only the Lonely	**257**
Sylvestris	**258**

PRIMITIVE	
Bosikappal	**259**
Chapeollo	**260**
Chichicaste	**261**
Cuba 4	**262**
Daule	**263**
Guácharo	**264**
Hyang Cho	**265**
Iztepeque	**266**
Little Cuba	**267**
Mopan Mayan	**268**
Mostrenco	**269**
Mountain Pima	**270**
Okinawa	**271**
Papante	**272**
Pretinho	**273**
Tabaco Colorado	**274**
Tabasqueño Prieto	**275**
Yumbo	**276**
NICOTIANA RUSTICA	
Aztec	**277**
Brasilia 7	**278**
Hasenkeyf	**279**
Isleta Pueblo	**280**
Karabaglar Rustica	**281**
Mohawk	**282**

Punche	**283**
Sacred Cornplanter	**284**
Sacred Wyandot	**285**
Shtambur	**286**
Sorotooskaia	**287**
Yellow 109	**288**

WILD

Clevelandii	**289**
Quadrivalvis	**290**

UNCLASSIFIED

Bravyi 200	**291**
Perique	**292**
Red Russian	**293**
Silver River	**294**

APPENDIX

Spacing Oriental Varieties	**295**

INDEX (alphabetical) — **297**

Other Books by the Author

Non-fiction by Robert C.A. Goff

> **Grow Your Own Cigars: growing, curing and finishing tobacco at home**
> **Blend Your Own Pipe Tobacco: 52 recipes with 52 color labels**
> **Ninety More Pipe Blends: 90 more recipes with 90 color labels**
> **How to Read a US Roadmap**
> **Climbing Out: Grand Canyon Hikes 1997-2006**
> **Just Walking Home: Appalachian Trail Hikes 1996-2013**
> **In the Ozone: collected essays, poems and non-fiction**
> **The Cigar Artistry of Marc Langanes: torcedor and photographer**
> **It Could Have Gone Either Way: the times I almost died**

Fantasy-fiction by Robert C.A. Goff

> **Ternaria: Legacy of a Careless Age**

Science-Fiction by Robert C.A. Goff

> **Impact Mitigation and other Science-Fiction Short Stories**

Fantasy-fiction by Robert C.A. Goff and Micah M.A. Goff

> The Counterspell Chronicle
> **Counterspell: Guardian of the Ruins**
> **Counterspell: The Second Law**
> **Counterspell: Age of Fools** [upcoming]

Acknowledgments

This book would not have been possible without the contributions of Paul Wicklund, of Northwood Seeds (in Spokane County, eastern Washington State). I know of no individual on the planet who has grown as many different varieties of tobacco, all the while selecting, harvesting and maintaining their seed. There are some national germplasm seed banks in a small number of countries which, as institutions, have grown more. But as an individual, Paul stands alone in this regard. When the number of tobacco varieties held in the Fair Trade Tobacco Forum seed bank reached over 400, the forum was no longer capable of required refreshment of the seed by forum volunteers. We turned to Paul, known by the user name of *skychaser* to other forum members. As the most experienced forum member at maintaining pure varietal tobaccos, Paul accepted the challenge of taking the seed bank into his safekeeping. He has generously allowed me to freely use his accumulated years of tobacco photos in this volume.

    I am indebted to Wallace Kemp for his assistance in finalizing the list of varieties that are presented here. Don Carey, of Whole Leaf Tobacco, and founder of the Fair Trade Tobacco Forum, as always, has provided his enthusiastic encouragement of the project. Many of the photos and metrics in this volume come from the tobacco section of the USDA ARS-GRIN database, maintained at the University of North Carolina. And many of those photos were the work of Jessica Nifong. Thank you.

R.C.A.G. (2022)

A tobacco field at Northwood Seeds

16   *Robert C.A. Goff*

Corojo 99

Introduction

There are many thousands of named varieties of tobacco plants, even if we include only *Nicotiana tabacum* varieties, commonly known as "smoking tobacco." In addition, there are over 70 other species in the genus *Nicotiana*, including *N. rustica* (cultivated by native peoples throughout North America for thousands of years), as well as a number of smokable, wild species, and non-smokable (i.e. potentially toxic) ornamentals and early ancestors of *N. tabacum*. In the United States, the Agricultural Research Service of the US Department of Agriculture Germplasm Resource Information Network (ARS-GRIN) maintains a genetic seed bank of tobacco varieties that number over 3000. Other countries have their own seed banks that contain additional varieties of tobacco.

Although it can be fun and rewarding to select exotic-sounding varieties of tobacco to grow at home, most home growers have particular uses in mind for their finished tobacco, like cigars, pipe, chew, snus, or cigarettes. Given the substantial time and labor involved in the process of growing tobacco at home, from germination all the way to finished tobacco and blending, this volume is an effort to present a reasonably limited selection of available plant varieties that may yield what the grower hopes to produce.

Take the 16th century advice of John Heywood:

I wyll neuer bye the pyg in the poke
Thers many a foule pyg in a feyre cloke

Select your varieties from a standpoint of knowledge of their potential, and avoid purchasing tobacco seed from unknown seed sellers. (It may or may not be what is advertised.)

I should add a word about tobacco USDA "market class", which was established during the late 19th century, and often based on production regions and their (then) typical market use or uses. You can consider the use class as a very crude guide for your own possible uses of tobacco. And the USDA (and ARS-GRIN) has perpetuated a number of errors in their class assignment. For example, the variety known as "Perique" was derived likely from a variety of red burley, resembles Hickory Pryor flue-cured plants during growth, and bears no resemblance at all to Oriental tobaccos, yet it remains classified as an Oriental. [In addition, you can make your own pressure-cured Perique using any variety of tobacco you wish. The variety name simply identifies the plants grown in St. James Parish, in Louisiana. The variety you choose for making Perique mostly determines the resulting nicotine content, more than the flavor and aroma.]

How many varieties should you grow in a single season? A reasonable limit for a first-time grower would be no more than six varieties. As the number of different varieties grown in a single season increases, the bookkeeping burden increases dramatically, and saps away the enjoyment. And an increased number of varieties inevitably means fewer instances of each variety, making assessment of characteristics more of a challenge.

An experienced home grower might wish to set aside a small garden allotment dedicated to growing one or two new varieties each year. I would say that a minimum of 4 instances of each variety should be grown. Making only a relatively small commitment to exploring new varieties can be both informative and fun. And the small number of plants involved will minimize any worries over a poor choice.

With regard to the classes, "cigar wrapper," "cigar binder" and "cigar filler", their determination is based mostly on the traditional market of the variety, rather than on characteristics of the plant or its leaves. Most varieties of cigar leaf of any of those three use classes can provide suitable wrappers, binders and filler leaf. Even long, narrow leaves with angular secondary veins can successfully wrap a cigar of any length, so long as its ring size (diameter) is less than about 44 (or 11/16 of an inch). So select your cigar varieties based on flavor, aroma, strength, productivity and ease of growing, rather than its market use class.

The "flue-cured" use class consists of varieties that are traditionally flue-cured, but these can also be successfully sun-cured. Air-curing these will result in quite smokable tobacco, but it will not resemble the golden, slightly acidic and sweet tobacco often used in pipe blends and cigarette blending. For similar reasons, most Oriental tobacco varieties are traditionally sun-cured, but also can be flue-cured successfully. When air-cured, Orientals often lose much of their floral character, but are still smokable tobacco.

The "dark" classes of tobacco tend to produce thick, sticky leaf that can be successfully air-cured or fire-cured. They all yield finished tobacco that is relatively high in nicotine and rich aromas.

For *Nicotiana rustica* varieties, keep in mind that their most notable feature, once cured and aged, is very high nicotine. (That makes them ideal for "ceremonial" purposes, but will certainly render blends made with them far higher in nicotine than the same blend without the *rustica*.)

The USDA definition of "primitive" is a variety that has apparently undergone little in the way of agronomic development and selection for desired traits. Many make wonderful finished tobacco, but at somewhat lower yields.

This book will present each of the selected tobacco varieties on its own, single page. Images of the entire plant, a single leaf, and in some instances the blossoms, will be provided if they are available. Specific information about each variety will include the kinds of data that may be useful to you in deciding if it is really what you have in mind. If you live in a growing area with a relatively short growing season, then "days to maturity" is meaningful for your ability to produce seed from your grow. *[Don't take the "days to maturity" too seriously. It can vary dramatically from region to region and from season to season.]* But most varieties (there are a few exceptions) can successfully produce mature leaf in just about any part of the globe, and at any land elevation. I make little attempt to subjectively describe flavors and aromas.

Information for each variety (in addition to photos):

- Class
- Typical uses
- Curing methods
- Days to maturity
- Height range
- Length and width of the 10th leaf
- Spacing between plants in a garden bed
- Narrative description of characteristics

Information on certain characteristics is lacking for some varieties. Where ARS-GRIN identifiers are available, they are given. Yield (ounces of cured leaf per plant) is often not readily available, nor is the nicotine content. Even among the 100+ varieties that I have personally grown, crucial photos and measurements are absent from my extensive data records. Ah! The photos I wish I had taken! The measurements I wish I had recorded!

In selecting multiple varieties to grow in an area where you might be concerned about plants shading one another, a selection of varieties of different general heights will enable you to place the shortest ones facing the direction of the sun (to the South in garden beds of the northern hemisphere, and to the North in beds of the southern hemisphere). The tallest varieties would go toward the opposite edge of the garden bed, and so forth.

Spacing of plants is based on my general experience. The values given are similar to "within row" gardening values. Space between rows is not given, since the layout of your bed will determine your needs. (Do you use a horse-drawn plow? A tractor? Need to walk between rows? Four staggered rows of identical spacing can be easily reached and maintained, if the width of the bed is limited to 5 feet, with adequate access to the perimeter. Most Orientals will grow to a huge size, if spaced widely, and lack the floral character that is typical of them. So for most Orientals, the surprisingly close spacing of 6-12 inches is recommended.

Finding "yield" data has been difficult, and reported yields in ounces of cured leaf per plant often vary widely by grower. Some of my entries for "yield" are wild guesses based on reports of yield per acre (kg/ha or lb/acre), with the loose estimate of 3000 plants per acre. So be skeptical of those yield values. [My own grows have sometimes produced yields of cured leaf per plant more than double the ARS-GRIN reported yield. Sometimes, half as much.] It is fair to say that lots of big leaves per plant yield more than fewer or smaller leaves per plant.

I hope that readers of this abbreviated "catalog" will not only find its content useful, but also an enjoyable browsing experience. Presenting all the snippets of *available* data for each variety in a single page should save you time. (Please excuse any blurry photos. They are the very best I could find.)

Flue-Cured   African Red   Flue-Cured

African Red is a bright leaf variety with white stemmed, light green leaves. A vigorous grower. The leaves air-cure to a light reddish brown. The smoke is mild and comparable to Virginia Gold. Air-cured and kilned leaf offer a mild, low-acidity cigarette blender that can also be used alone. Original seed donated to the USDA from Transvaal, South Africa in 1975, (named, "RT," for red tobacco).

Days to Maturity: 80 days
Spacing: 24-36 inches
Plant Height: 84-96 inches
Leaf Length: 28 inches
Leaf Width: 12 inches
Leaf Count: 28 leaves

Home-grown African Red puro

Comments:
Original seed donated to the USDA from Japan in 1935.

ARS-GRIN
PI 405003
TI 166
Cultivar Name: "RT", "Red Tobacco"
Yield:
Nicotine: 2.98%

Photos: Northwood Seeds, Northwood Seeds, ARS-GRIN, RCAG

Flue-Cured　　Awa　　Flue-Cured

Awa is a bright leaf variety from Japan, acquired in 1935. Suckering is low before topping.

Days to Maturity: 50-65 days
Spacing: 24-36 inches
Plant Height: 60-72 inches
Leaf Length: 24-26 inches
Leaf Width: 12-14 inches
Leaf Count: 22

Comments:

ARS-GRIN
PI 405003
TI 1609
Yield: 3 ounces of cured leaf per plant
Nicotine: 2.33%

Photos: ARS-GRIN, ARS-GRIN

Flue-Cured   Bamboo Shoot   Flue-Cured

Bamboo Shoot is a bright leaf variety. The leaves air cure to a light yellow or golden brown. Bamboo Shoot is mild to smoke. The seed was originally collected in Ghizhou, China, and donated to ARS-GRIN in 1988.

Days to Maturity: 80-85 days
Spacing: 24-36 inches
Plant Height: 96 inches
Leaf Length: 22-23 inches
Leaf Width: 9-10 inches
Leaf Count: 14-16

Comments:

ARS-GRIN
PI 518745
TI 1719
Yield:
Nicotine:

Photos: Northwood Seeds, ARS-GRIN

Flue-Cured   Banana Leaf   Flue-Cured

Banana Leaf is a bright variety, developed from the original Orinoco type tobacco,. It was the first of the many Virginian type bright leafs developed. Leaves ripen about 2 weeks after flowering.

Days to Maturity: 55-60 days
Spacing: 24-30 inches
Plant Height: 72 inches
Leaf Length: 26-30 inches
Leaf Width: 12-16 inches
Leaf Count: 17-20

Comments:

ARS-GRIN
PI 552298
TC 235
Yield: 3+ ounces of cured leaf per plant
Nicotine:

Photos: ARS-GRIN, Northwood Seeds

Flue-Cured   Big Gem   Flue-Cured

Big Gem is an heirloom bright leaf variety. A tried and true variety that is a very good producer. An excellent choice for a cigarette blend. Air cures to a light brown color.

During the late 19th century, some considered this to have been derived from a variety of burley.

Days to Maturity: 63 days
Spacing: 24-30 inches
Plant Height: 60-84 inches
Leaf Length: 24-30 inches
Leaf Width: 12-18 inches
Leaf Count: 18

Comments:

ARS-GRIN
PI 552343
TC 241
Yield: 2½ ounces of cured leaf per plant
Nicotine:

Photos: Northwood Seeds, ARS-GRIN, Northwood Seeds

Flue-Cured   Bonanza   Flue-Cured

Bonanza is an heirloom, bright variety. A stabilized cross between White Burley and Yellow Orinoco flue cure, with characteristics of both parents. It was one of the first varieties released by the Oxford tobacco station (late 1920s or early 30s). There are two "bonanzas" listed in GRIN. only one of them is the original variety (PI 552300).

Days to Maturity: 50-63 days
Spacing: 24-36 inches
Plant Height: 48-72 inches
Leaf Length: 25-30 inches
Leaf Width: 11-12 inches
Leaf Count: 18

Comments:

ARS-GRIN
PI 552300
TC 242
Yield: 3-4 ounces of cured leaf per plant
Nicotine:

Photos: ARS-GRIN, Northwood Seeds, Northwood Seeds

Flue-Cured Brown & Williams Low Nicotine Flue-Cured

A bright leaf variety developed by the Brown and Williams tobacco company for a cigarette tobacco with a low nicotine content. 1991 donation to ARS-GRIN.

Days to Maturity: 53-70 days
Spacing: 24-36 inches
Plant Height: 53-90 inches
Leaf Length: 25-30 inches
Leaf Width: 11-14 inches
Leaf Count: 20

Comments:

ARS-GRIN
PI 552598
TC 246
Yield: 3 ounces of cured leaf per plant
Nicotine:

Photos: ARS-GRIN, ARS-GRIN, Northwood Seeds

Flue-Cured Bucak Flue-Cured

Bucak is a bright variety developed in Turkey from a flu-cure type tobacco imported in the 1930's from the US. It grows large heavy leaves densely spaced on the stalk. It tolerates heavy rains and wind well and will withstand early fall frosts with little or no damage. It air cures easily to a light brown.

Days to Maturity: 50 days
Spacing: 24-36 inches
Plant Height: 60 inches
Leaf Length: 22-26 inches
Leaf Width: 12-14 inches
Leaf Count: 20

Comments:

Photos: Northwood Seeds, Northwood Seeds.

Flue-Cured   401 Cherry Red   Flue-Cured

401 Cherry Red is a bright variety. Moderate suckering. Leaves air cure to a light reddish brown color. Cherry Red is a long time favorite as a pipe tobacco and its mild taste makes it excellent in a cigarette blend.

Days to Maturity: 56-75 days
Spacing: 24-36 inches
Plant Height: 50-84 inches
Leaf Length: 21-24 inches
Leaf Width: 10-15 inches
Leaf Count: 18-26

Comments: Slightly resistant to root-knot nematode and leaf spot.

ARS-GRIN
PI 552572
TC 227
Yield: 2 ounces of cured leaf per plant
Nicotine:

Photos: ARS-GRIN, ARS-GRIN, ARS-GRIN

Flue-Cured Coker 213 Flue-Cured

Coker 213 was developed by the Coker Seed Company in the 1960's. The leaves have the classic Virginian type shape and are large. It has excellent curability.

Coker 213 has high resistance to black shank, and good resistance to bacterial wilt and fusarium wilt. It also has tolerance to brown spot.

Days to Maturity: 58-70 days
Spacing: 24-36 inches
Plant Height: 56-72 inches
Leaf Length: 25-30 inches
Leaf Width: 9-18 inches
Leaf Count: 21

Pedigree
Date released: 1970
Coker 319/Coker 139
Crop Science Registration. CV-47, TOBACCO. Issued: 01 Nov 1970.

Comments:

ARS-GRIN
PI 552475
TC 268
Yield: 4 ounces of cured leaf per plant
Nicotine:

Photos: Northwood Seeds, Northwood Seeds, ARS-GRIN

Flue-Cured — Coker 371-Gold — Flue-Cured

Coker 371 Gold was released by Novartis Seeds, Inc. in 1986. It was developed from crosses involving Speight G-28, NC 82 and several breeding lines. Air-cures easily to a good yellow orange color.

Coker 371-Gold has high resistance to black shank and moderate resistance to Granville wilt and brown spot. It has also been reported to be resistant to cyst nematode.

Days to Maturity: 65-77 days
Spacing:
Plant Height: 54-60 inches
Leaf Length:
Leaf Width:
Leaf Count: 19

Pedigree
Speight G-28/Coker 354//CB-139/F-105//Speigh G-28/Coker 354/3/NC 82
U.S. Plant Variety Protection
PVP 8700049 1987, certificate expired

Comments:

ARS-GRIN
PI 552524
TC 276
Yield:
Nicotine:

Photos: ARS-GRIN, ARS-GRIN, ARS-GRIN

Flue-Cured   Costello Negro   Flue-Cured

Costello Negro is a bright variety acquired by the ARS-GRIN from Flandes, Tolima, Colombia in 1966. Closely spaced leaves. It has a sweet mild flavor with a slightly nutty taste, and is useful for cigarette or pipe blends. It can be used in a blend, or on its own. The leaves air-cure to a light brown to a dark reddish brown. They sun-cure particularly well.

Days to Maturity: 60-70 days
Spacing: 24-36 inches
Plant Height: 66 inches
Leaf Length: 26 inches
Leaf Width: 12 inches
Leaf Count: 31

Comments:

ARS-GRIN
PI 318757
TI 1491
Yield: 4 ounces of cured leaf per plant
Nicotine: 2.4%

Photos: Northwood Seeds, ARS-GRIN, ARS-GRIN

Crimean

Flue-Cured

Flue-Cured

Crimean is a large-leaved, columnar shaped bright variety, with oval shaped leaves and down turned edges. Relatively resistant to the tomato spotted wilt virus.

Days to Maturity: 60-70 days
Spacing: 24-36 inches
Plant Height: 60-72 inches
Leaf Length: 14-16
Leaf Width: 8
Leaf Count: 16-20

Pedigree (Peremozhets 83 x Nicotiana sylvestris)

Comments:

Yield:
Nicotine:

Photos: Northwood Seeds, Northwood Seeds

Flue-Cured   Delgold   Flue-Cured

Delgold is a flue-cured variety from Canada. It is a well known, bright leaf variety, still considered one of the better yielding flue-cured varieties available for commercial tobacco production. It is fast growing, and produces large, wide, heavy grade, light green leaves. Flue-cures to a dark orange color

Days to Maturity: 64-75 days
Spacing: 24-36 inches
Plant Height: 60-72 inches (topped at 40 inches)
Leaf Length: 25 inches
Leaf Width: 12 inches
Leaf Count: 18

Comments:

GRIN Canada
CN 39635

Yield:
Nicotine: 2.2%

Photos: Northwood Seeds

Flue-Cured   Dixie Bright 27   Flue-Cured

Dixie Bright 27 is a flue-cured variety developed in the 1960's. Light green leaves, with good yield and heavy weight. Leaves air cure to a light yellow brown. The flavor is light and mild.

Days to Maturity: 61-77
Spacing: 24-36 inches
Plant Height: 47-58 inches
Leaf Length: 20-27 inches
Leaf Width: 11-16 inches
Leaf Count: 17-22

Pedigree
Date released: 1949
TI 448A/400/Yellow Special A
Crop Science Registration. CV-13, TOBACCO. Issued: 01 Jan 1966.

Comments:

ARS-GRIN
PI 552355
TC 288
Yield: 4 ounces of cured leaf per plant
Nicotine:

Photos: Northwood Seeds, ARS-GRIN, ARS-GRIN

Flue-Cured   **Frog Eye Orinoco**   **Flue-Cured**

Frog Eye Orinoco is one of several varieties derived in part from the original Orinoco, from what is today's Venezuela. [The introduction of Orinoco tobacco into colonial Virginia replaced their failing European trade in *Nicotiana rustica* with the far more successful export of *N. tabacum,* assuring the colony's future.] It is used in cigarette and pipe blends.

Days to Maturity: 53-70
Spacing: 24-36 inches
Plant Height: 47-60 inches
Leaf Length: 24-26 inches
Leaf Width: 12-14 inches
Leaf Count: 16-18

Comments:

ARS-GRIN
PI 552633
TC 296
Yield: 2¼ ounces of cured leaf per plant
Nicotine:

Photos: ARS-GRIN, ARS-GRIN, ARS-GRIN

Flue-Cured Gold Dollar Flue-Cured

Gold Dollar is an heirloom bright leaf variety. Early maturing. Commonly used in cigarette and pipe blends. Air cures to a light brown.

Gold Dollar is a selection from Jamaica seeds provided to Coker in 1928 by the Oxford Tobacco Research Station.

Days to Maturity: 50-55
Spacing: 24-36 inches
Plant Height: 37½-54 inches
Leaf Length: 23-24 inches
Leaf Width: 7½-10½ inches
Leaf Count: 18

Comments:

ARS-GRIN
PI 552310
TC 299
Yield: 1-2 ounces of cured leaf per plant
Nicotine:

Photos: ARS-GRIN, ARS-GRIN, ARS-GRIN

Flue-Cured   Gold Leaf   Flue-Cured

Gold Leaf is a bright variety with very good yields. It grows with closely spaced leaves, and has excellent uniformity between plants which makes it easy to manage. Suckering is very low. The leaves air-cure to a light golden brown.

Can be air-cured, rather than flue-cured.

Days to Maturity: 50-65
Spacing: 24-36 inches
Plant Height: 33½-44 inches
Leaf Length: 22-23½ inches
Leaf Width: 8-12 inches
Leaf Count: 14-20

Comments:

ARS-GRIN
PI 552643
TC 300
Yield: 1½ ounces of cured leaf per plant
Nicotine:

Photos: ARS-GRIN, ARS-GRIN, ARS-GRIN

Flue-Cured   Gold Leaf Orinoco   Flue-Cured

Gold Leaf Orinoco (or Cold Leaf Orinoco) is a bright variety that collected by Raymond Stadelman in 1937, in Peru. It has a pyramidal shape. The flavor of Gold Leaf Orinoco is similar to the dark Virginian types of tobacco, with the upper leaves being the strongest. It is useful for cigarette and pipe blending. Gold Leaf Orinoco has a has a much higher nicotine content than most bright varieties.

Days to Maturity: 43-65
Spacing: 24-36 inches
Plant Height: 35-42 inches
Leaf Length: 15½-27½ inches
Leaf Width: 6-12½ inches
Leaf Count: 14-17

Comments:

ARS-GRIN
PI 119869
TI 1073
Yield: 2½-4 ounces of cured leaf per plant
Nicotine: 3.99%

Photos: Northwood Seeds, ARS-GRIN, ARS-GRIN

Flue-Cured Golden Harvest Flue-Cured

Golden Harvest is a bright variety developed by the Coker Seed Company in the 1970's. Useful for cigarette and pipe blending. The leaves are large, with good over all yields and curability. Suckering is low.

Golden Harvest is root-knot nematode tolerant.

Days to Maturity: 50-59
Spacing: 24-36 inches
Plant Height: 56-84 inches
Leaf Length: 23-30 inches
Leaf Width: 15-18 inches
Leaf Count: 19

Intellectual Property Rights
Crop Science Registration. CV-76, TOBACCO. Issued: 01 Jan 1975.
Pedigree
Date released: 1948; Gold Dollar/400

Comments:

ARS-GRIN
PI 552399
TC 302
Yield: 2 ounces of cured leaf per plant
Nicotine:

Photos: ARS-GRIN, Northwood Seeds, ARS-GRIN

Flue-Cured   Golden Wilt   Flue-Cured

Golden Wilt is a bright variety with high resistance to Granville wilt, Fusarium wilt, and good resistance to black shank. It is a vigorous grower, with large, closely space leaves up the stalk. It performs well in areas with short growing seasons. The leaves ripen shortly after blooming begins. It is a heavy producer. The leaves easily air-cure to a light golden yellow. It's mild flavor and smoothness make it useful for cigarette and pipe blending.

Days to Maturity: 59-69
Spacing: 24-36 inches
Plant Height: 52-84 inches
Leaf Length: 20-22 inches
Leaf Width: 11-12 inches
Leaf Count: 19-21

Pedigree
Date released: 1949. Virginia Bright Leaf/TI 448A
Intellectual Property Rights
Crop Science Registration. CV-75, TOBACCO. Issued: 01 Jan 1975.

Comments:

ARS-GRIN
PI 552393
TC 303
Yield: 2½ ounces of cured leaf per plant
Nicotine:

Photos: Northwood Seeds, Northwood Seeds

Flue-Cured — Goyano — Flue-Cured

Goyano is a bright variety from Brazil, acquired by ARS-GRIN in 1936. It has a very high nicotine content for a bright leaf variety.

Days to Maturity: 47-67
Spacing: 24-36 inches
Plant Height: 40-60 inches
Leaf Length: 16½-24 inches
Leaf Width: 9-12 inches
Leaf Count: 18-20

Comments:

ARS-GRIN
PI 117669
TI 814
Yield: ¾-3 ounces of cured leaf per plant
Nicotine: 5.13%

Photos: ARS-GRIN, ARS-GRIN

Flue-Cured   Helena   Flue-Cured

Helena is an heirloom bright variety. The leaves air-cure or sun-cure easily to a golden yellow color. It's leaves ripen earlier than many other bright varieties, and ripen as the plant reaches bloom. Helena has a smooth, light flavor. Useful for cigarette or pipe blending.

Days to Maturity: 60-65
Spacing: 24-36 inches
Plant Height: 72-84 inches
Leaf Length: 21-28 inches
Leaf Width: 12-18 inches
Leaf Count: 16-18

Comments:

Yield: 4 ounces of cured leaf per plant
Nicotine:

Photos: Northwood Seeds, Northwood Seeds

Flue-Cured Hickory Pryor Flue-Cured

Hickory Pryor is an heirloom bright variety. The leaves air cure to a medium golden brown. It's mild smoke and flavor make it useful for cigarette or pipe blending.

Days to Maturity: 54-70
Spacing: 24-36 inches
Plant Height: 48-70 inches
Leaf Length: 30 inches
Leaf Width: 12 inches
Leaf Count: 19-20

Comments:

ARS-GRIN
PI 552314
TC 309
Yield: 2-4 ounces of cured leaf per plant
Nicotine:

Photos: Northwood Seeds, ARS-GRIN, ARS-GRIN

Flue-Cured Jaffna Flue-Cured

Jaffna is a bright variety that originated in British Ceylon, now known as Sri Lanka, and was acquired by ARS-GRIN in 1936. It has a very high nicotine for bright tobacco. The dark colored leaves lighten in color and turn slightly yellow as they ripen.

Days to Maturity: 54-63
Spacing: 24-36 inches
Plant Height: 49-72 inches
Leaf Length: 25-30 inches
Leaf Width: 12-18 inches
Leaf Count: 17-20

Comments:

ARS-GRIN
PI 113985
TI 501
Yield: 4-5 ounces of cured leaf per plant
Nicotine: 6.15%

Photos: ARS-GRIN, ARS-GRIN

Flue-Cured   Lemon Bright   Flue-Cured

Lemon Bright is a bright variety developed in the 1950's. It has a light mild flavor and is useful for cigarette and pipe blending.

Days to Maturity: 56-60
Spacing: 24-36 inches
Plant Height: 48-72 inches
Leaf Length: 26-30 inches
Leaf Width: 13-18 inches
Leaf Count: 17-18

Comments:

ARS-GRIN
PI 552317
TC 324
Yield: 1¾-3 ounces of cured leaf per plant
Nicotine:

Photos: ARS-GRIN, ARS-GRIN, ARS-GRIN

Lizard Tail Orinoco

Flue-Cured   **Flue-Cured**

Lizard Tail Orinoco is a bright variety that is more strongly flavored than most. It is useful for fuller-flavored cigarette or pipe blending. The dark green leaves are thick and closely spaced on the stalk. They air-cure to a rich brown.

Days to Maturity: 55-63
Spacing: 24-36 inches
Plant Height: 48 inches
Leaf Length: 20-26 inches
Leaf Width: 6-9 inches
Leaf Count: 14-16

Comments:

ARS-GRIN
PI 552377
TC 477
Yield:
Nicotine:

Photos: ARS-GRIN, ARS-GRIN, ARS-GRIN

Flue-Cured   NC 82   Flue-Cured

NC 82 is a bright variety. High resistance to black shank and is resistant to bacterial wilt, fusarium wilt, and black root rot. NC 82 has large thick leaves with very good cured leaf quality. May flower prematurely.

Days to Maturity: 60-70
Spacing: 24-36 inches
Plant Height: 36-48 inches
Leaf Length: 26 inches
Leaf Width: 9½-12 inches
Leaf Count: 16-18

Pedigree: Coker 319/NC 6129/3/(Virginia 21/Bottom Special//8038-3)
Intellectual Property Rights
Crop Science Registration. CV-84, TOBACCO. Issued: 01 Sep 1981.

Comments:

ARS-GRIN
PI 551311
TC 356
Yield:
Nicotine:

Photos: Northwood Seeds, ARS-GRIN

Ostrolist

Flue-Cured

Ostrolist (formally, 'Ostrolist B-27-47') is a bright variety developed in the 1960's in Bulgaria. Suckering is low.

Days to Maturity: 54-60
Spacing: 24-36 inches
Plant Height: 54-72 inches
Leaf Length: 18-26 inches
Leaf Width: 11-14 inches
Leaf Count: 18-20

Comments:

ARS-GRIN
PI 321712
TI 1495
Yield: 2-4 ounces of cured leaf per plant
Nicotine: 3.07%

Photos: ARS-GRIN, ARS-GRIN, ARS-GRIN

Flue-Cured   Oxford 207   Flue-Cured

Oxford 207 is a bright leaf variety that was developed in North Carolina. Air cures to a golden yellow color. Exhibits good yield and quality characteristics.

Flue-cured tobacco combining high level of resistance to bacterial wilt (*Pseudomonas solanacearum*) with high level of resistance to race 0 black shank (*Phytophthora nicotianae*). Also has resistance to races 1 and 3 of southern root knot nematode (*Meloidogyne incognita*). Resistant to fusarium wilt (*Fusarium oxysporum*). Susceptible to the predominant virus diseases of flue-cured tobacco.

Days to Maturity: 60-77
Spacing: 24-36 inches
Plant Height: 60 inches
Leaf Length: 20-25 inches
Leaf Width: 6-9 inches
Leaf Count: 16-20

Pedigree
Date released: 1997. Coker 319/K 399
Intellectual Property Rights
Crop Science Registration. CV-114, TOBACCO. Issued: 01 Jan 1999.
U.S. Plant Variety Protection: 11/04/1997. Application Abandoned

Comments:

ARS-GRIN
PI 601992
TC 632
Yield:
Nicotine:

Photos: ARS-GRIN, ARS-GRIN

Flue-Cured   Paris Wrapper   Flue-Cured

Paris Wrapper is an heirloom bright leaf variety that is a vigorous early season grower. The leaves are a very light green with white stems. Air cures to a light golden brown. It has a light mild flavor and is a good choice for cigarette tobacco. Though a flue-cure variety, it was once popular as a bright, claro cigar wrapper.

Days to Maturity: 56-65
Spacing: 24-36 inches
Plant Height: 44-47 inches
Leaf Length: 21-30 inches
Leaf Width: 20 inches
Leaf Count: 17-20

Comments:

ARS-GRIN
PI 552328
TC 378
Yield: 3 ounces of cured leaf per plant
Nicotine:

Photos: ARS-GRIN, ARS-GRIN, ARS-GRIN

Flue-Cured   **Polish**   **Flue-Cured**

Polish is an early maturing bright leaf variety developed in Italy (accession in 1963). Leaves are closely spaced on the stalk.

Resistant to veinal necrosis. Moderately resistant to black root rot (*Thielaviopsis basicola*). Susceptible to downy mildew (*Peronospora tabacina*).

Days to Maturity: 48-56
Spacing: 24-36 inches
Plant Height: 43-48 inches
Leaf Length: 18-25 inches
Leaf Width: 10-16 inches
Leaf Count: 18

Comments:

ARS-GRIN
PI 292195
TI 1441
Yield: 2-3 ounces of cured leaf per plant
Nicotine: 2.58%

Photos: ARS-GRIN, ARS-GRIN, ARS-GRIN

Reams 158

Flue-Cured

Reams 158 is a high yielding bright variety. Leaves are light colored and are closely spaced on the stalk. Suckering is very low. Air-cures to a light yellow/brown. Reams 158 was developed by Reams Seed Company. This variety has moderate resistance to black shank and low resistance to Granville wilt.

Days to Maturity: 50-65
Spacing: 24-36 inches
Plant Height: 60 inches
Leaf Length: 14-20 inches
Leaf Width: 6-9 inches
Leaf Count:

Pedigree: McNair 944/Hicks

Comments:

ARS-GRIN
PI 552744
TC 397
Yield:
Nicotine:

Photos: Northwood Seeds

Flue-Cured   Silk Leaf   Flue-Cured

Silk Leaf is an old heirloom Virginian variety which has regained popularity among growers in recent years. It is a good producer. Used mainly as a cigarette tobacco for its mild flavor, or as a pipe blend.

Seeds originally obtained by EG Moss from local tobacco growers in Gulliford County, NC.

Days to Maturity: 43-70
Spacing: 24-36 inches
Plant Height: 50-72 inches
Leaf Length: 20-23 inches
Leaf Width: 12 inches
Leaf Count: 15-20

Comments:

ARS-GRIN
PI 552331
TC 404
Yield: 1½-2 ounces of cured leaf per plant
Nicotine:

Photos: ARS-GRIN, ARS-GRIN, ARS-GRIN

Flue-Cured   Southern Beauty   Flue-Cured

Southern Beauty is an heirloom bright variety which is a quick and vigorous grower. Gives very good yields. Air-cures to a golden yellow.

Days to Maturity: 50-60
Spacing: 24-36 inches
Plant Height: 47-72 inches
Leaf Length: 25-30 inches
Leaf Width: 13-16 inches
Leaf Count: 17-19

Comments:

ARS-GRIN
PI 552333
TC 412
Yield: 3 ounces of cured leaf per plant
Nicotine:

Photos: Northwood Seeds, ARS-GRIN, ARS-GRIN

Flue-Cured   **Stolak 17**   **Flue-Cured**

Stolak 17 is a bright variety developed in former Serbia and Montenegro. (Donated to ARS-GRIN in 1978.) Produces a fine leaf structure and texture, and is a vigorous grower. It has a low nicotine content and mild flavor similar to Virginia Golds. Useful for cigarette and pipe blending.

Susceptible to blue mold.

Days to Maturity: 65-90
Spacing: 24-36 inches
Plant Height: 57-84 inches
Leaf Length: 17-20 inches
Leaf Width: 9-10 inches
Leaf Count: 26-28

Comments:

ARS-GRIN
PI 423619
TI 1622
Yield:
Nicotine: 1.83%

Photos: Northwood Seeds, ARS-GRIN, ARS-GRIN

Flue-Cured   Ternopolski 7   Flue-Cured

Ternopolski 7 is a Russian bright leaf variety developed from the Soviet Large Leaf series by the Ternopol seed station in Ukraine. Suckering is very low. The ripe, creamy yellow leaves air cure easily to a bright yellow or light golden brown. Ternopolski 7 has high yields and it's mild flavor makes it an excellent choice for use in cigarettes or pipe blends.

Disease resistance: tobacco mosaic virus, Peronosporosis (downy mildew).

Days to Maturity: 65-**107**
Spacing: 24-36 inches
Plant Height: 52 inches
Leaf Length: 14-24 inches
Leaf Width: 7-14 inches
Leaf Count: 22-26

Comments:

Yield:
Nicotine: 1.2-1.6%

Photos: Northwood Seeds, Northwood Seeds, Northwood Seeds

Flue-Cured — Ternopolski 14 — Flue-Cured

Ternopolski 14 is a Russian "large leaf", bright variety, developed by the Ternopol seed station in Ukraine. Suckering is very low. Best if primed in 3 pickings for the highest quality air-cured leaf. Ternopolski 14 air-cures easily to a bright yellow or golden brown. It has a mild flavor, and is useful for cigarette or pipe blending.

Resistance: tobacco mosaic virus and Peronosporosis (downy mildew).

Days to Maturity: 72-75
Spacing: 24-36 inches
Plant Height: 82-96 inches
Leaf Length: 17-24 inches
Leaf Width: 10-14 inches
Leaf Count: 24-26

Comments:

Yield:
Nicotine: 1.2%

Photos: Northwood Seed, Northwood Seed, Northwood Seed

Flue-Cured   Thailand   Flue-Cured

Thailand bright leaf tobacco. The exact name of this strain is not known. It appears to be a "Virginia Gold" type of tobacco. It is a well developed strain that is uniform in its growth, with low suckering, making it an easy to manage plant. It air-cures golden yellow to light golden brown.

Days to Maturity: 55
Spacing: 24-36 inches
Plant Height: 60 inches
Leaf Length: ~18-20 inches
Leaf Width: ~9 inches
Leaf Count: ~16-18

Comments:

Yield: 2-3 ounces of cured leaf per plant
Nicotine:

Photos: Northwood Seeds, Northwood Seeds

Flue-Cured   **Virginia 15**   **Flue-Cured**

Virginia 15, a bright variety, is a light, aromatic cigarette and pipe tobacco. Stated to be resistant to "most" diseases. [?] Virginia 15 is a late maturing variety. Often air-cured. From western Ukraine (Transcarpathia).

Days to Maturity: 90-117
Spacing: 24-36 inches
Plant Height: 54-60 inches
Leaf Length: 12-22 inches
Leaf Width: 6-14 inches
Leaf Count: 22

Comments:

Yield:
Nicotine: 0.95%

Photos: Northwood Seeds, Northwood Seeds, Northwood Seeds

Flue-Cured   Virginia 24   Flue-Cured

Virginia 24 is a bright variety that produces a large leafed, high grade leaf tobacco with little suckering. Said to be resistant to "most" diseases. Air cures easily to a light golden brown. Often air-cured.

Days to Maturity: 65-70
Spacing: 24-36 inches
Plant Height: ~60 inches
Leaf Length: ~18 inches
Leaf Width: ~10 inches
Leaf Count: 14-16

Comments:

Yield:
Nicotine:

Photos: Northwood Seeds, Northwood Seeds

Flue-Cured   **Virginia 116**   **Flue-Cured**

Virginia 116 is a bright variety, developed at Virginia Tech. Easy to air cure and dries a bright golden yellow. It is mild to smoke and is useful for cigarette or pipe blending. Resistance moderate to black shank (*Phytophthora parasitica*), Granville wilt (*Pseudomonas solanacearum*) and brown spot (*Alternaria alternata*).

Days to Maturity: 65
Spacing: 24-36 inches
Plant Height: 36-56 inches
Leaf Length: 20-25½ inches
Leaf Width: 9½-12 inches
Leaf Count: 19

Pedigree
Released: 1990. NC 82/Coker 319
Intellectual Property Rights
Crop Science Registration. CV-101, TOBACCO. Issued: 01 Jul 1991.

Comments:

ARS-GRIN
PI 543922
TC 609
Yield:
Nicotine:

Photos: ARS-GRIN, ARS-GRIN, ARS-GRIN

Flue-Cured   Virginia 647   Flue-Cured

Virginia 647, a bright variety, is originally from Poland. It is an early maturing variety, and air-cures easily to a light golden brown.

Days to Maturity: 55-60
Spacing: 24-36 inches
Plant Height: 56 inches
Leaf Length: 10-26 inches
Leaf Width: 6-14 inches
Leaf Count: 14-15

Comments:

Yield:
Nicotine:

Photos: Northwood Seeds

Flue-Cured   Virginia Bright Leaf   Flue-Cured

Virginia Bright Leaf is an heirloom bright variety. Leaves begin to ripen as the plant reaches bloom. Air-cures easily to a light golden brown.

Days to Maturity: 55
Spacing: 24-36 inches
Plant Height: 46-72 inches
Leaf Length: 20-25½ inches
Leaf Width: 8-12 inches
Leaf Count: 17-20

Comments:

ARS-GRIN
PI 552385
TC 446
Yield: 2¼-3 ounces of cured leaf per plant
Nicotine:

Photos: Northwood Seeds, Northwood Seeds, ARS-GRIN

Flue-Cured   **Virginia Gold**   **Flue-Cured**

Virginia Gold is a well known heirloom variety dating back well over 50 years. It grows with low suckering. The light green leaves turn a light yellow when ripe. Virginia Gold is a root rot resistant flue-cured variety.

Days to Maturity: 55-56
Spacing: 24-36 inches
Plant Height: 44-55 inches
Leaf Length: 24-30 inches
Leaf Width: 14-18 inches
Leaf Count: 17-18

Comments:

ARS-GRIN
PI 552334
TC 447
Yield: 2-3 ounces of cured leaf per plant
Nicotine:

Photos: ARS-GRIN, ARS-GRIN, Northwood Seeds

Flue-Cured Vesta 64 Flue-Cured

Vesta 64 is a bright variety. Leaves air-cure to a light golden brown. It is a vigorous grower, but prolonged cool early season weather can cause above average suckering.

Days to Maturity: 53-60
Spacing: 24-36 inches
Plant Height: 47-60 inches
Leaf Length: 23-26 inches
Leaf Width: 11-12 inches
Leaf Count: 17

Pedigree White Stem Orinoco/FL 301//White Stem Orinoco/3/Yellow Special

Comments:

ARS-GRIN
PI 552772
TC 442
Yield: 2 ounces of cured leaf per plant
Nicotine:

Photos: ARS-GRIN, ARS-GRIN, ARS-GRIN

Flue-Cured   White Gold   Flue-Cured

White Gold is South Carolina heirloom bright variety developed in the 1950's by the Coker Seed Company. Leaves ripen shortly after blooming occurs, making it a good choice for short season growers. It air-cures to a light brown.

Days to Maturity: 55-60
Spacing: 24-36 inches
Plant Height: 44-47 inches
Leaf Length: 22-30 inches
Leaf Width: 14-16 inches
Leaf Count: 18

Pedigree
Date released: 1950. Huggins Golden Yellow/402

Comments:

ARS-GRIN
PI 552400
TC 449
Yield: 2½-3 ounces of cured leaf per plant
Nicotine:

Photos: ARS-GRIN, Northwood Seeds, ARS-GRIN

Flue-Cured   **White Mammoth**   **Flue-Cured**

White Mammoth is a bright variety that grows quickly, and matures early. Suckering is low and the leaves air-cure easily. A good choice for short growing seasons.

Days to Maturity: 55-56
Spacing: 24-36 inches
Plant Height: 40-54 inches
Leaf Length: 22-24 inches
Leaf Width: 11-12 inches
Leaf Count: 15-16

Comments:

ARS-GRIN
PI 552336
TC 450
Yield: 1¾ ounces of cured leaf per plant
Nicotine:

Photos: ARS-GRIN, ARS-GRIN, ARS-GRIN

Flue-Cured White Stem Orinoco Flue-Cured

White Stem Orinoco is an heirloom bright variety which originated from the early Virginia Orinoco's (introduced to colonial Virginia from what is now Venezuela). It is stronger flavored than most bright leaf varieties and is a good choice for a fuller flavored cigarette or pipe blend. It matures early. The dark green leaves are thick and closely spaced on the stalk. They air-cure to a rich brown. Suckering is moderate.

Days to Maturity: 51-61
Spacing: 24-36 inches
Plant Height: 44-46½ inches
Leaf Length: 23-24 inches
Leaf Width: 11-14 inches
Leaf Count: 16-17

Comments:

ARS-GRIN
PI 552337
TC 451
Yield: 2-3 ounces of cured leaf per plant
Nicotine:

Photos: Northwood Seeds, ARS-GRIN

Flue-Cured Yellow Gold Flue-Cured

Yellow Gold is a bright variety that produces among the larger leaves of any bright leaf type. The leaves air-cure to a light brown.

Days to Maturity: 50-55
Spacing: 24-36 inches
Plant Height: 48-72 inches
Leaf Length: 23-30 inches
Leaf Width: 13-18 inches
Leaf Count: 16-18

Comments:

ARS-GRIN
PI 552781
TC 452
Yield: 2-3 ounces of cured leaf per plant
Nicotine:

Photos: ARS-GRIN, Northwood Seeds, ARS-GRIN

Yellow Leaf

Flue-Cured   **Flue-Cured**

Yellow Leaf is a bright variety, imported from Ukraine. It produces good yields of leaf. Air-cures to a light yellow brown color.

Days to Maturity: 60
Spacing: 24-36 inches
Plant Height: 72 inches
Leaf Length: 24-26 inches
Leaf Width: 16 inches
Leaf Count: ~16-18

Comments:

Yield:
Nicotine:

Photos: Northwood Seeds, Northwood Seeds

Flue-Cured   Yellow Orinoco   Flue-Cured

Yellow Orinoco is an heirloom bright variety which originated from Virginia Orinoco. Suckering is low, and is less than with White Stemmed or Frog Eye Orinoco. Leaves air-cure to a light brown.

Days to Maturity: 50-56
Spacing: 24-36 inches
Plant Height: 42-60 inches
Leaf Length: 24-26 inches
Leaf Width: 12-14 inches
Leaf Count: 15-16

Comments:

ARS-GRIN
PI 552783
TC 455
Yield: 2-3 ounces of cured leaf per plant
Nicotine:

Photos: ARS-GRIN, ARS-GRIN

Flue-Cured   Yellow Pryor   Flue-Cured

Yellow Pryor an heirloom bright variety useful in both cigarette and pipe blending. It grows with little suckering. It is a very good producer. Leaves air-cure to a light brown. A hardy plant with good wind and frost resistance.

Days to Maturity: 50-55
Spacing: 24-36 inches
Plant Height: 37-48 inches
Leaf Length: 24-25 inches
Leaf Width: 12 inches
Leaf Count: 17-19

Comments:

ARS-GRIN
PI 552339
TC 456
Yield: 4½ ounces of cured leaf per plant
Nicotine:

Photos: Northwood Seeds, ARS-GRIN, ARS-GRIN

Burley — Baldío Vera — Burley

Baldío Vera is a unique variety of burley from the Extremadura region of Spain. *[Baldío = "wasteland". Vera is east of Placencia, Spain.]* It is considered a burley variety. It produces a full-size plant with large leaves. It looks very much like a white-stem burley, with pale stalks and veins, and a quick color-cure to a light golden brown. It may be a burley relative, but grown in isolation for a half-millennium in Spain's Extremadura, it does not exhibit a characteristic "burley" taste and aroma. It is fairly mild, with a slight pepper edge. This may be an ancient landrace tobacco, brought back to Spain by the early Conquistadores, since many of them called the Extremadura home.

The large leaves of Baldío Vera easily air-cure to a uniform, light brown. It is most suitable for cigarette and pipe blending.

Days to Maturity: 66
Spacing: 24-36 inches
Plant Height: 50-60 inches
Leaf Length: 25 inches
Leaf Width: 15 inches
Leaf Count: 19

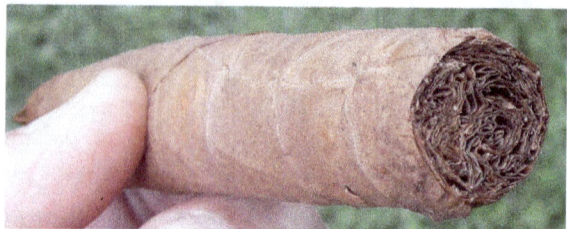

Home-grown Balío Vera puro

Comments:

Yield: 4-5 ounces of cured leaf per plant
Nicotine:

Photos: all RCAG

Burley 9

Burley

Burley 9 is a high-yielding, late-season variety for air-curing. Developed in western Ukraine (Transcarpathia). Leaves are light green, and turn yellow as they ripen. It air-cures to a light golden brown. Burley 9 is drought resistant and said to be "resistant to disease."

Days to Maturity: 65-102
Spacing: 24-36 inches
Plant Height: 67 inches
Leaf Length: 14-24 inches
Leaf Width: 8-16 inches
Leaf Count: 24-16

Comments:

Yield:
Nicotine: 1.6%

Photos: Northwood Seeds, Northwood Seeds, Northwood Seeds

Burley 21

Burley 21 is an heirloom Burley variety that is a long time favorite of growers (released in 1955). It is a reliable producer of large heavy leaf. It does well in a wide range of climates. The leaves make a strong, full flavored smoke. Burley 21 is commonly used in blending cigarettes and pipe tobacco.

In addition to resistance to wildfire and TMV, Burley 21 has moderate to low resistance to black root rot and has tolerance to lesion nematodes.

Days to Maturity: 59-71
Spacing: 24-36 inches
Plant Height: 46½-56 inches
Leaf Length: 23½ inches
Leaf Width: 11 inches
Leaf Count: 20-21

Pedigree
Date released: 1955. TL 106, Kentucky 16, Greeneville 5, Kentucky 41A, Kentucky 56/Greeneville 18

Intellectual Property Rights
Crop Science Registration. CV-21, TOBACCO. Issued: 01 Nov 1966.

Comments:

ARS-GRIN
PI 552363
TC 7
Yield: 3 ounces of cured leaf per plant
Nicotine:

Photos: ARS-GRIN, ARS-GRIN

Burley — Burley 64 — Burley

Burley 64 is a columnar plant. It is a white stemmed burley with large light green leaves that turn bright yellow as they ripen. It gives good yields with very little suckering, and cures easily, either stalk hung or primed. Burley 64 is resistant to black root rot, tobacco mosaic virus, wildfire, fusarium wilt, and black shank.

Days to Maturity:
Spacing: 24-36 inches
Plant Height: 60-72 inches
Leaf Length: 14-20 inches
Leaf Width: 6-9 inches
Leaf Count: 14-18

Pedigree
Date released: 1973. 62-231-25H/62-486-25H

Intellectual Property Rights
Crop Science Registration. CV-60, TOBACCO. Issued: 01 Jul 1974.

Comments:

ARS-GRIN
PI 551251
TC 11
Yield:
Nicotine:

Photos: Northwood Seeds, Northwood Seeds

| Burley | Chillard's White Angel Leaf | Burley |

This white-stem burley variety is of unknown pedigree. It was grown and identified near Chilliwack, British Columbia (Canada) in 2014. It's unusual characteristic is that the lower leaves turn a cream-colored white as they mature, no doubt due to a genetic defect in chlorophyll metabolism. Nonetheless, all of the leaves easily air-cure to a lovely, medium brown. They provide a medium-strength burley for cigarette and pipe blending. They can also be used for a light-to-medium colored cigar wrapper.

Days to Maturity: 66
Spacing: 30-36 inches
Plant Height: 60-72 inches
Leaf Length: 24-28 inches
Leaf Width: 13 inches
Leaf Count: 26

Bottom and top leaf of the same plant

Comments:
The delightful color of the lower leaf is simply a visual curiosity for the grower, with no impact on the resulting, cured leaf.

Yield:
Nicotine:

Photos: all RCAG

Burley   Golden Burley   Burley

Golden Burley is a medium flavored Burley with excellent curability. The leaves turn a bright lemon yellow when ripe. Air cures to a light buck skin brown. The smoke is flavorful, yet mild. Requires less aging time than many Burleys.

Days to Maturity: 58-88
Spacing: 24-36 inches
Plant Height: 38-60 inches
Leaf Length: 16-30 inches
Leaf Width: 10-12 inches
Leaf Count: 17-23

Comments:

ARS-GRIN
PI 552644
TC 14
Yield: 1½ ounces of cured leaf per plant
Nicotine:

Photos: ARS-GRIN, ARS-GRIN, ARS-GRIN

Burley — Green Brior — Burley

Green Brior is a full flavored, heavy producing heirloom Burley that is a long time favorite of growers. It grows light green leaves. It produces well in a wide range of growing conditions. Low suckering.

Days to Maturity: 62-70
Spacing: 24-36 inches
Plant Height: 45½-59 inches
Leaf Length: 21½-25 inches
Leaf Width: 11-14 inches
Leaf Count: 19-20

Comments:

ARS-GRIN
PI 552645
TC 40
Yield: 3½ ounces of cured leaf per plant
Nicotine:

Photos: ARS-GRIN, ARS-GRIN

Burley — Harrow Velvet — Burley

Harrow Velvet is a medium flavored Burley (developed in Canada) with excellent curability and a short aging time. It has a columnar plant form with tightly spaced leaves which are uniform in size. Almost no suckering. Leaves turn a golden yellow as they ripen. Leaf air-cures to a medium buckskin brown. An excellent plant for priming or to cut and hang whole. Very good wind resistance.

Days to Maturity: 53-75
Spacing: 24-36 inches
Plant Height: 36-39 inches
Leaf Length: 20-24 inches
Leaf Width: 9½-14 inches
Leaf Count: 15-22

Comments:

ARS-GRIN
PI 552650
TI TC 45
Yield: 3 ounces of cured leaf per plant
Nicotine:

Photos: ARS-GRIN, ARS-GRIN, RCAG, Northwood Seeds

| Burley | Kelly Burley | Burley |

Kelly Burley is an heirloom white-stem variety that tends to ripen uniformly. Historically, it was used to make plug tobacco. It is useful for cigarette and pipe blending. Color-cures easily with air-curing. Grows slowly after transplant, but then grows vigorously after 1 month.

Days to Maturity: 47-60
Spacing: 24-36 inches
Plant Height: 32-55 inches
Leaf Length: 17-28 inches
Leaf Width: 8-12 inches
Leaf Count: 14-19

Comments:

ARS-GRIN
PI 552671
TC 51
Yield: 2 ounces of cured leaf per plant
Nicotine:

Photos: ARS-GRIN, RCAG

Burley — KY 15 — Burley

KY15 is a white stem, high yielding Kentucky Burley. Highly resistant to tobacco mosaic virus, wild-fire, and black root rot. Medium to high resistance to Fusarium wilt and tolerance to TEV.

KY15 is a columnar plant with large closely spaced leaves. Few suckers. Leaves turn yellow as they ripen, curling down around the edges. Air-cures easily as primed leaf or stalk-hung. The leaves dry to a light orange brown. Mature plants have some frost resistance.

note bumblebee

Days to Maturity: 60-65
Spacing: 24-36 inches
Plant Height: 48 inches
Leaf Length: 18-20 inches
Leaf Width: 8-12 inches
Leaf Count: 16-18
Pedigree—Date released: 1978. KY 14/Burley 49//KY 14/3/Burley 21/4/KY 10

Intellectual Property Rights
Crop Science Registration. CV-82, TOBACCO. Issued: 01 Jul 1978.

Comments:

ARS-GRIN
PI 551279
TC 58
Yield:
Nicotine:

Photos: ARS-GRIN, ARS-GRIN, ARS-GRIN

Burley   KY 17   Burley

KY 17 is a heavy producing, white-stemmed burley. The light green leaves are unusually large. Pyramidal shaped plant. KY 17 grows slower in the first half of the season with its growth spurt occurring 2-3 week later than many other varieties. This is a trait common to several white-stem burleys. But it quickly catches up and surpasses other types by the end of its second month. The leaves turn yellow on the edges and have yellow mottling when ripe. It is easy to air-cure and is an excellent plant for priming or whole-stalk curing. The leaves air cure to a light golden brown. It is useful for blending with bright leaf varieties in cigarette or pipe blends.

Days to Maturity: 70
Spacing: 24-36 inches
Plant Height: 60-72 inches
Leaf Length: 20-36 inches
Leaf Width: 9-24 inches
Leaf Count: 14-18
Pedigree: modified backcross scheme involving Beinhart 1000, Bel 66-11, Burley 37, Burley 49, and Va 509
Intellectual Property Rights: Crop Science Registration. CV-83, TOBACCO. Issued: 01 Jul 1978.

Comments:

ARS-GRIN
PI 552674
TC 60
Yield: 6-8 ounces of cured leaf per plant
Nicotine: 4.0%

Photos: ARS-GRIN, ARS-GRIN, Northwood Seeds

| Burley | **KY 190** | Burley |

KY 190 is a dark, strongly flavored Kentucky Burley, often fire-cured. Plants are categorized as dark, fire-cured type (22 and 23). Released for its good yield of high quality leaf and disease resistance. Cured leaf rated good to excellent with acceptable leaf chemistry. High resistance to TMV, wildfire (*Pseudomonas tabaci*) and black root rot (*Thielaviopsis basicola*). Medium resistance to races R0 and R1 of black shank.

Days to Maturity: 65
Spacing: 24-36 inches
Plant Height: 36 inches
Leaf Length: 20-25½ inches
Leaf Width: 9½-12 inches
Leaf Count: 14-15

Pedigree
Date released:1988. KY 171*6/TXF 811

Intellectual Property Rights
Crop Science Registration. CV-99, TOBACCO. Issued: 01 Jul 1989.

Comments:

ARS-GRIN
PI 527338
TC 574
Yield:
Nicotine: 5.75% (total alkaloid content)

Photos: ARS-GRIN, ARS-GRIN, ARS-GRIN

| Burley | KY 8635 | Burley |

KY 8635 is a white-stem Burley variety. It produces large, uniformly sized leaves with little to no suckering. Leaves turn yellow as they ripen. Very easy to air-cure and an excellent plant for priming. Air-cures to an orange brown color. Resistant to root knot nematodes (*Meloidogyne incognita*). Tolerates light frost well.

Days to Maturity: 55-70
Spacing: 24-36 inches
Plant Height: 72 inches
Leaf Length: 16-24 inches
Leaf Width: 10-12 inches
Leaf Count: 14-16

Pedigree—Date released: 1987. NC 95*4/KY 17

Intellectual Property Rights
Crop Science Registration. GP-25, TOBACCO. Issued: 01 Jan 1988.

Comments:

ARS-GRIN
PI 511341
TC 75
Yield:
Nicotine:

Photos: ARS-GRIN, ARS-GRIN, ARS-GRIN

LI Burley 21

Burley | **Burley**

LI Burley 21 is a large, heavy producing (low to intermediate nicotine) white-stem Burley. The leaves are a light green with down turned edges that turn yellow as they ripen. LI Burley 21 is a late maturing variety. It is a genetically stable line, with low-intermediate (LI) levels of alkaloids. It was derived by selfing and selection within segregated generations of a cross between Burley 21 and LA Burley 21.

Days to Maturity: 75-80
Spacing: 24-36 inches
Plant Height: 48-96 inches
Leaf Length: 20-24 inches
Leaf Width: 11-14 inches
Leaf Count: 23-36

Pedigree: Burley 21/LA Burley 21

Intellectual Property Rights
Crop Science Registration. GP-27, TOBACCO. Issued: 01 Jan 1988.

Comments:

ARS-GRIN
PI 511343
TC 81
Yield:
Nicotine: ~1.2% (total alkaloids)

Photos: ARS-GRIN, Northwood Seeds, Northwood Seeds

| Burley | Moldovan 456 | Burley |

Moldovan 456 is a tall, stand up burley, with a growth habit similar to TN 90 or Burley 21. It is a heavy producer. The upturned leaves close-up tight to the stalk at dusk. Moldovan 456 has good wind resistance and is much more resistant to tipping than many other tall burleys. The plants shed water well during heavy rains and dry quickly helping to preventing mildew growth in humid areas.

Suckering is low, with most plants producing none before flowering. Leaves begin to ripen two weeks or more before reaching bloom, making the entire plant harvestable in about 90 days from transplanting. Moldovan 456 air-cures easily to a bright yellow brown and is suitable for either priming or stalk-curing. Useful for making cigarette or pipe blends.

Resistance Peronosporosis, Tomato Spotted Wilt Virus, Cucumber Mosaic Virus and black root rot.

Days to Maturity: 75-110
Spacing: 36 inches
Plant Height: 55-67 inches
Leaf Length: 16-25 inches
Leaf Width: 8-16 inches
Leaf Count: 34-40

Comments:

Yield: 6-7 ounces of cured leaf per plant
Nicotine: 1.6-3.0%

Photos: Northwood Seeds, Northwood Seeds

Burley Monte Calme Yellow (Jaune) Burley

Monte Calme Yellow (also known as Monte Calme Jaune) is a burley variety developed in Switzerland. The leaves are a dark green with light colored stems. It produces some of the largest and heaviest leaf found in Burley varieties. It's blossoms are very light pink, almost white. Mature plants have good resistance to light frosts showing little or no damage to the leaves.

[This should not be confused with Monte Calme Brown (Brun), which is a Swiss-developed Havana type.]

Days to Maturity: 65-70
Spacing: 24-36 inches
Plant Height: 60-72 inches
Leaf Length: 30 inches
Leaf Width: 20 inches
Leaf Count: 12-14

Comments:

Yield:
Nicotine:

Photos: Northwood Seeds, D. Carey, Northwood Seeds

Burley — NB-11 — Burley

NB-11 is a productive burley type that was developed by grower selection from unknown seed in New Brunswick, Canada, in 2005, and was stabilized in 2011.

[Growing out, I got 19 distinctly different plants. Most were junk. But this one was exceptional...large leaves, mild, very sturdy stalks.]

Can be primed or stalk-cut and stalk-hung for curing. (Leaf maturation may require 40 or more days beyond blossom.) It air-cures easily to a rich, medium brown. Suitable for cigarette or pipe blending. This has been a grower favorite burley on the Fair Trade Tobacco forum.

Days to Maturity: 52 (leaf maturity at ~95 days)
Spacing: 24-36 inches
Plant Height: 42 inches
Leaf Length: 22 inches
Leaf Width: 13 inches
Leaf Count: 16-18

Comments:

Yield: 4½ ounces of cured leaf per plant
Nicotine:

Photos: RCAG, RCAG

Burley — Sobolchskii — Burley

Sobolchskii is a fast growing and early maturing, light flavored Burley. Light green leaves. It cures easily, either primed or stalk hung to a light golden brown. Sobolchskii is useful for cigarette and pipe blendending. Leaves ripen and turn yellow as the plants reach maturity.

Days to Maturity: 60-65
Spacing: 24-36 inches
Plant Height: 60-72 inches
Leaf Length: 20-24 inches
Leaf Width: 14 inches
Leaf Count: 16

Comments:

Yield:
Nicotine:

Photos: Northwood Seeds, Northwood Seeds

Burley   Sobolchskii 33   **Burley**

Sobolchskii 33 is a fast growing and very early maturing, light flavored burley, useful for cigarette tobacco or pipe blending. The very large, light green leaves turn yellow as the plant reaches maturity and begins to bloom. Sobolchskii 33 has some of the largest leaves of any burley type. The leaf is easy to air-cure. It is an excellent choice for growers with very short seasons. It is the standard type of tall Sobolchskii grown in Ukraine since 1999.

Days to Maturity: 50-60
Spacing: 24-36 inches
Plant Height: 72 inches
Leaf Length: 28 inches
Leaf Width: 22-24 inches
Leaf Count: 16-25

Comments:

Yield:
Nicotine: 1.8%

Photos: Northwood Seeds, Northwood Seeds, Northwood Seeds

Burley — Sobolchskii 193 — Burley

Sobolchskii 193 is a "cigarette-variety" burley imported from the Ukraine. It is a tall, columnar plant with light green leaves. It is easy to air-cure, and has a smooth, mild taste. Leaves cure to a reddish yellow-brown. Useful for cigarette or pipe blending.

Days to Maturity: 60-94 (mid-late)
Spacing: 24-36 inches
Plant Height: 84 inches
Leaf Length: 15 inches
Leaf Width: 7 inches
Leaf Count: 24-26

Comments:

Yield: 2½-3 ounces of cured leaf per plant
Nicotine: 1.8%

Photos: Northwood Seeds, Northwood Seeds

Burley · Spectrum · Burley

Spectrum is a white-stem burley variety developed in western Ukraine (Transcarpathia). The light green leaves turn a mottled yellow when ripe. It is drought resistant, and resistant to adverse weather conditions. It has a mild flavor with a medium level of nicotine. It air-cures easily. Useful for cigarette and pipe blending.

Days to Maturity: 60-73
Spacing: 24-36 inches
Plant Height: 48-72 inches
Leaf Length: 20-26 inches
Leaf Width: 12-20 inches
Leaf Count: 24-26

Pedigree: (Kurtie x Bigleaf 38 x Yellowleaf 36)

Comments:

Yield:
Nicotine:

Photos: Northwood Seeds, Northwood Seeds

Burley — Symbol 4 — Burley

Symbol 4 is a burley variety imported from western Ukraine (Transcarpathia). Leaves are packed densely on the stem. Symbol 4 is a heavy producer with good yields. The light green oval shaped leaves become yellow at the tips and edges which spreads across the leaf when ripe. The leaves begin to ripen before the plant reaches bloom, making it a reasonable choice for short season areas.

Symbol 4 air-cures to a bright yellow gold, with an excellent burning quality. It has a stronger richer taste than bright leaf, having a hint of Dutch tobacco flavor and aroma to the smoke, and is useful for cigarette or pipe blending.

Days to Maturity: 50-84
Spacing: 24-36 inches
Plant Height: 63-72 inches
Leaf Length: 16 inches
Leaf Width: 9 inches
Leaf Count: 24-28

Pedigree (Sobolchsky 193 x Jubilee 8 x Virginia American)

Comments:
Harvesting of leaves should be started when the leaf turns completely yellow, with the appearance of light spots, which is typical for the variety.

Yield:
Nicotine:

Photos: Northwood Seeds, Northwood Seeds

Burley — TN 86 — Burley

TN 86 was released by the Tennessee Ag. Experiment Station in 1986. TN 86 is a medium-to-late-maturing cultivar, that has more leaves and a more upright growth habit than most other burley cultivars. Widely adaptable. The air-cured leaf is generally reddish-tan. Useful for cigarette and pipe blending.

Disease resistance:
TN 86 has high resistance to TVMV, black root rot (*Theilaviopsis basicola*), and wildfire (*Pseudomonas tabaci*); medium high resistance to TEV; medium resistance to Race 0 and Race 1 black shank; and is resistant to most strains of PVY. TN 86 is more sensitive to blue mold than are other burley tobacco varieties.

Days to Maturity: 72-80 (harvest 30 days after bloom)
Spacing: 36 inches
Plant Height: 54 inches
Leaf Length: 31 inches
Leaf Width: 13 inches
Leaf Count: 22-26

Pedigree: Burley 49 x PVY-202

Intellectual Property Rights:
Crop Science Registration. CV-95, TOBACCO. Issued: 01 Mar 1987.

Comments:

ARS-GRIN
PI 552522
TC 82

Yield: ~8 ounces of cured leaf per plant
Nicotine: 4.2%

Photos: Northwood Seeds, ARS-GRIN, Northwood Seeds

TN 86 LC

Burley

TN 86 LC is a burley variant that tends to convert less nicotine into nornicotine (which may be transformed into TSNAs during curing). TSNAs are an important health risk with inhaled or oral tobacco use. This low converter trait *is variable from plant to plant*, and is predictive of LC only in seed collected from test-verified low converters in the F_1 (first hybrid) generation. Home growers cannot collect seed from this variety, and expect subsequent crops to be low converters, without laboratory testing.

LC varieties are not "low nicotine" varieties.

Days to Maturity: 80
Spacing: 36 inches
Plant Height: 54-60 inches
Leaf Length: 19-31 inches
Leaf Width: 10-14 inches
Leaf Count: 22

Comments:

Yield: 6-8 ounces of cured leaf per plant
Nicotine: 4+%

Photos: Northwood Seeds

Burley   TN 90   Burley

TN 90 is one of the most widely grown tobaccos in the world. It is an excellent Burley tobacco. It's earlier maturity and smaller stalk offer an advantage over TN 86 to some growers. The light green leaves air-cure easily, both primed or stalk hung. TN 90 performs well in a wide variety of climates. Today, most US commercial growers must use a low converter variant (e.g. TN 90 LC) to meet tightening industry standards for reduced nornicotine.

High resistance to TMV, Tobacco Vein Mottling Virus, Black Root Rot, Wildfire. Medium resistance to Race 0 and 1 of Black Shank. Resistance to Potato Virus Y varies. Medium to high resistance to most PVY strains in U.S.

Days to Maturity: 70
Spacing: 36 inches
Plant Height: 48-60 inches
Leaf Length: 20-24 inches
Leaf Width: 14-16 inches
Leaf Count: 20-22

Pedigree: Burley 21*2//Burley 49/PVY 202, F11

Intellectual Property Rights
Crop Science Registration. CV-100, TOBACCO. Issued: 01 May 1991.

Comments:

ARS-GRIN
PI 543792
TC 586
GR 141

Yield: 6-8 ounces of cured leaf per plant
Nicotine:

Photos: Northwood Seeds, Northwood Seeds

Burley — TN 90 LC — Burley

TN 90 LC is a burley variant that tends to convert less nicotine into nornicotine (which may be transformed into TSNAs during curing). TSNAs are an important health risk with inhaled or oral tobacco use. This low converter trait *is variable from plant to plant*, and is predictive of LC only in seed collected from test-verified low converters in the F_1 (first hybrid) generation. Home growers cannot collect seed from this variety, and expect subsequent crops to be low converters, without laboratory testing. LC varieties are not "low nicotine" varieties.

Disease resistance: moderate to black shank, some tolerance to blue mold and black root rot, and resistance to common virus diseases.

Days to Maturity: 70
Spacing: 36 inches
Plant Height: 48-60 inches
Leaf Length: 20-24 inches
Leaf Width: 14-16 inches
Leaf Count: 20-22

Comments:
Good cured leaf color.

Yield: 6-8 ounces of cured leaf per plant
Nicotine:

Photos: Northwood Seeds, Northwood Seeds

Burley — Virginia 509 — Burley

Virginia 509 Burley is a heavy producing variety. The leaves are closely spaced on the stalk. Its lower growing plant form gives it good wind resistance and is more resistant to blow down than many taller Burleys. The leaves turn a golden yellow when ripe. It air-cures easily, both primed or stalk hung, and is useful for cigarette and pipe blending.

Released to commercial seed producers in 1967 in the F8 generation. Disease resistance of Virginia 509 is high for wildfire, moderate black shank, moderate for black root rot, and low for Fusarium wilt.

Days to Maturity: 50-60
Spacing: 24-36 inches
Plant Height: 48-60 inches
Leaf Length: 22 inches
Leaf Width: 12-14 inches
Leaf Count: 15-16

Comments:

ARS-GRIN
PI [not assigned]
TC 84
Yield:
Nicotine:

Photos: ARS-GRIN, ARS-GRIN, Northwood Seeds

Yellow Twist Bud

Burley | **Burley**

Yellow Twist Bud is an heirloom variety of white-stem Burley. It produces few suckers and its pyramidal plant form with closely spaced leaves give it very good resistance to wind and inclement weather. The leaves turn a light yellow when ripe and are easy to air-cure. Good for cigarette and pipe blending.

Days to Maturity: 60-79
Spacing: 24-36 inches
Plant Height: 40½-44½ inches
Leaf Length: 20-30 inches
Leaf Width: 8-12 inches
Leaf Count: 10-13

Comments:

ARS-GRIN
PI 552784
TC 88
Yield: 1½-2 ounces of cured leaf per plant
Nicotine:

Photos: ARS-GRIN, ARS-GRIN, Northwood Seeds

Cigar   **Ahus**   **Cigar**

Ahus is a fast growing and very early maturing tobacco from Sweden. It is ideal for areas with very short growing season. The leaf can be harvested at 40-45 days. Ahus can be used for a cigar or pipe blending, and is often used in making snus.

[Åhus is a well-preserved, medieval town in Sweden, though tobacco is no longer grown there.]

Days to Maturity: 30-40 (harvest 40-50 days)
Spacing: 24-36 inches
Plant Height: 30 inches
Leaf Length: 15 inches
Leaf Width: 7-8 inches
Leaf Count: 8-12

Comments:

Yield:
Nicotine:

Photos: Northwood Seeds, Northwood Seeds

Cigar — Amarello Rio Grande — Cigar

Amarello Rio Grande (Amarello Rio Grande do Sul No.1) is an heirloom cigar filler variety from Uruguay. Sharply pointed leaves which ripen as the plants begin blooming. Air-cures to a light brown. Useful for cigar filler and pipe blending.

Days to Maturity: 57-90
Spacing: 24-36 inches
Plant Height: 47-59 inches
Leaf Length: 22½-31 inches
Leaf Width: 9-12 inches
Leaf Count: 14-28

Comments:

PI 404949
TI 74
(GRIN Market Class: 'Other')

Yield: 5 ounces of cured leaf per plant
Nicotine: 1.93%

Photos: ARS-GRIN, Northwood Seeds

Cigar — Amarillo Parado — Cigar

Amarillo Parado ("standing yellow") is a "Criollo" (a native) type cigar filler from the Dominican Republic.

[The three chief varieties of Criollo tobacco in the DR (in the mid 20th century) were Amarillo Parado, Amarillo Planchado, and Jagua. These are characterized by leaves of thicker, coarser character, with more prominent lateral veins, that meet the midrib at sharp angles, in comparison with the Olor types. Amarillo Parado was highly appreciated, because it is resistant to disease and returns high yields.]

Useful as cigar filler or binder.

Amarillo Parado holds its leaves fairly upright and straight throughout growth, until ripening.

Days to Maturity: 73-93
Spacing: 24-36 inches
Plant Height: 60 inches
Leaf Length: 16-20 inches
Leaf Width: 6-9 inches
Leaf Count: 26

GRIN accession note: *"Highly resistant to black shank and leaf diseases. Good cigar filler quality."*

Comments:

ARS-GRIN
PI 377898
TI 1583
Yield: 3½ ounces of cured leaf per plant
Nicotine: 1.09%

Photos: RCAG, ARS-GRIN, RCAG

Cigar — Besuki H382 (Ambulu) — Cigar

Besuki H382 (Ambulu) is a variety of Besuki cigar wrapper leaf grown in the Ambulu area of Timor Leste. The seed was collected by Anton Eise deVries in 2016. It is grown commercially there. Plants appear dark green until maturation. Lugs should be primed. Stalk-harvested 18 days after topping. Good for cigar wrappers, binders and filler. This appears to be the same general variety as Besuki H382 (Kesilir).

Days to Maturity: 70
Spacing: 24-36 inches
Plant Height: 50 inches
Leaf Length: 17 inches
Leaf Width: 9½ inches
Leaf Count: 16

Comments:

Yield:
Nicotine:

Photos: all RCAG

| Cigar | Besuki H382 (Kesilir) | Cigar |

Besuki H382 (Kesilir) is a variety of Besuki cigar wrapper leaf grown in the Kesilir area of Timor Leste. The seed was collected by Anton Eise deVries in 2016. It is grown commercially there. Plants appear dark green until maturation. Lugs should be primed. Stalk-harvested 18 days after topping. Good for cigar wrappers, binders and filler. This appears to be the same general variety as Besuki H382 (Ambulu).

Days to Maturity: 70
Spacing: 24-36 inches
Plant Height: 51 inches
Leaf Length: 19 inches
Leaf Width: 11½ inches
Leaf Count: 19

Comments:

Yield:
Nicotine:

Photos: all RCAG

Cigar — Besuki (Java) — Cigar

Besuki (Java) is a variety of Besuki cigar wrapper leaf grown from the seed labeled "Java Besuki". Lugs should be primed. Stalk-harvest 18 days after topping. Good for cigar wrappers. *[This is distinctly different in taste and aroma from "Sumatra" cigar wrapper, which is from the Deli Sumatra leaf variety. It is also distinctly different from the Ambulu and Kesilir Besuki.]*

Days to Maturity: 65-73
Spacing: 24-36 inches
Plant Height: 40-57 inches
Leaf Length: 23 inches
Leaf Width: 13½ inches
Leaf Count: 19

Comments:

Yield:
Nicotine:

Photos: Northwood Seeds, Northwood Seeds, Northwood Seeds

Cigar   **Brasil Dunkel**   **Cigar**

Brasil Dunkel (Brazil Dark) is a dark brown, aromatic Brazilian cigar tobacco with an even burn. Air-cured primed or stalk-cut. Used as cigar fillers, binders and wrappers, as ingredients for pipe and cigarette blending, and as the basis for Bavarian snuff tobacco (Schmalzler). It blends well with other cigar tobaccos. The seed is commercially available from tabakanbau.de. (The specific varietal name is not documented. It is perhaps derived from Mata Norte.) Seed produces some variants of plant characteristics.

Days to Maturity: 60
Spacing: 24-36 inches
Plant Height: 48 inches
Leaf Length: 22 inches
Leaf Width: 11 inches
Leaf Count: 24

Air-curing lugs

Comments:

Yield:
Nicotine:

Photos: all RCAG

Colombian Garcia

Cigar — **Cigar**

Colombian Garcia is a tall, late maturing cigar variety. It also appears to be sensitive to daylight period (actually the length of the dark period), growing much taller, and producing a bud head much later in the season, if exposed to nighttime lighting. Colombian Garcia is classed by ARS-GRIN as a cigar filler, due to its prominent, angular secondary veins. It is useful as cigar filler, binder and even wrapper. The finished tobacco is flavorful and slightly edgy, benefiting from greater aging and rest prior to use.

Days to Maturity: 89
Spacing: 24-36 inches
Plant Height: 81 inches
Leaf Length: 19-24½ inches
Leaf Width: 10-12½ inches
Leaf Count: 20-30

Comments:

ARS-GRIN
PI 405672
TI 1457
Yield: 4½ ounces of cured leaf per plant
Nicotine: 2.04%

Photos: ARS-GRIN, ARS-GRIN, RCAG, RCAG

Cigar   **Comstock Spanish**   **Cigar**

Comstock Spanish is an heirloom variety classed as a cigar binder, but it also makes an excellent wrapper and flavorful filler. One of the oldest tobacco varieties grown in Wisconsin. It is said to have been brought to the state in 1871 from Massachusetts, and maintained for years by the Pomeroy family of Edgerton. The leaves have good elasticity when cured, and droop downward with down turned edges when ripe.

Days to Maturity: 43-50
Spacing: 24-36 inches
Plant Height: 40-54 inches
Leaf Length: 18½-26 inches
Leaf Width: 12-14 inches
Leaf Count: 15-22

Comments:

ARS-GRIN
PI 552437
TC 89
Yield: 2 ounces of cured leaf per plant
Nicotine:

Photos: Northwood Seeds, ARS-GRIN, RCAG

Cigar — Connecticut 49 — Cigar

Connecticut 49 is a Connecticut Shade cigar wrapper type. It requires shade-growing (beneath 40% shade cloth) to be useful as a thin wrapper leaf. Sun-grown, it will produce thicker, much smaller leaves that may or may not be useful as cigar filler. CT 49's performance is similar to the older, Connecticut 15, but with leaves of greater elasticity, finer veins, and improved smoking taste.

[Connecticut 49 (Barwell) is quite similar, with a slightly earlier maturation, fractionally larger leaves and a marginal improvement in yield. PI 552618 TC 185]

Days to Maturity: 52-57
Spacing: 36 inches
Plant Height: 56-57 inches
Leaf Length: 19-20 inches
Leaf Width: 9-12 inches
Leaf Count: 18-19

Pedigree: AST/Connecticut G4

Comments:

ARS-GRIN
PI 551287
TC 184
Yield: 1½-2 ounces of cured leaf per plant
Nicotine:

Photos: ARS-GRIN, ARS-GRIN, ARS-GRIN

Cigar — Connecticut Broadleaf — Cigar

Connecticut Broadleaf is a fast maturing cigar wrapper tobacco. It is widely used for maduro cigar wrapper and binder, imparting its unique taste. Since CT Broadleaf is highly susceptible to blue mold, it should be planted in full, all-day sun, and planted widely enough to avoid the large leaves shading its CT Broadleaf neighbors. It air-cures to a deep brown.

Days to Maturity: 46-50
Spacing: 36 inches
Plant Height: 40-48 inches
Leaf Length: 23-30 inches
Leaf Width: 13-16 inches
Leaf Count: 12-13

[Amusing Fact: the leaf photo shown here is the actual photo from which the Fair Trade Tobacco Forum logo was created.]

Comments:

ARS-GRIN
PI 552619
TC 186
Yield: 2½ ounces of cured leaf per plant
Nicotine:

Photos: ARS-GRIN, ARS-GRIN, RCAG

Connecticut Shade

Cigar

Connecticut Shade is a cigar wrapper variety specifically developed (during the start of the 20th century) to be grown beneath shade cloth (~40% shade). Properly shade-grown, it produces very thin and large leaves. The shade-grown stalks may easily reach 8 feet or more, and require a supporting rope extending from the top of the shade framework. The support rope is gradually wound around the stalk as the plant grows taller. Sun-grown CT Shade will also be relatively tall, but produce thicker, smaller leaves that are not particularly inviting for use as cigar wrapper. Sun-grown plants do not usually require support.

Days to Maturity: 48-67
Spacing: 24-36 inches
Plant Height: 41-112 inches (taller shade-grown)
Leaf Length: 17-30 inches (longer shade-grown)
Leaf Width: 10-16 inches (wider shade-grown)
Leaf Count: 18-29 (higher shade-grown)

Comments:
ARS-GRIN
PI 552621
TC 188
Yield: 1½-3 ounces of cured leaf per plant
Nicotine:

Photos: Northwood Seed, ARS-GRIN, RCAG

Cigar — Coroja (Cuba) — Cigar

Coroja (Cuba) is an earlier cigar variety (Assigned to ARS-GRIN in 1976. The collection date is not documented.) along the path to developing Corojo 99 from the original Vuelta Abajo variety. It produces a reasonable yield of medium-size leaf, which cures to a satisfying cigar leaf. It is useful as wrapper, binder and filler.

ARS-GRIN incorrectly classes this variety as "Oriental". It is unquestionably a cigar type.

Days to Maturity: 35-58
Spacing: 24-36 inches
Plant Height: 36-56 inches
Leaf Length: 11½-19 inches
Leaf Width: 5-12 inches
Leaf Count: 12-19

Comments:

ARS-GRIN
PI 405643
TI 1373
Yield: 1½-2 ounces of cured leaf per plant
Nicotine: 2.13%

Photos: RCAG, ARS-GRIN, RCAG

Cigar **Corojo (Honduras)** **Cigar**

Corojo (Honduras) is a variety of cigar leaf that was being grown commercially in Honduras, when Anton Eise deVries collected the seed there in 2016. It is not listed by ARS-GRIN. The plant generally resembles Coroja (Cuba) in growth and productivity. It is useful as cigar wrapper, binder, and filler. It air-cures easily to a rich, medium brown leaf, with the square venation pattern desirable in wrappers.

Days to Maturity: 58
Spacing: 24-36 inches
Plant Height: 43-47 inches
Leaf Length: 17 inches
Leaf Width: 10 inches
Leaf Count: 19

Comments:

Yield:
Nicotine:

Photos: RCAG, RCAG

Corojo 99 (Cuba)

Corojo 99 (Cuba) is from seed collected within Cuba's Vuelta Abajo in 2015. Yield is excellent. The leaf easily color-cures to a soft, medium-brown, and is excellent as cigar wrapper, binder and filler. Puro cigars of just this variety provide a balanced, flavorful, medium-strength smoke. Tensile strength is good, and the burn is excellent, even for upper leaf (ligero). The lower leaves can be primed, while the remainder of the stalk can be stalk-cut, and stalk-cured in the shed. This variety is a good choice for a single variety, home cigar leaf grow. Tip leaf (corona) offers intense flavors and aromas.

Days to Maturity: 64-68
Spacing: 24-36 inches
Plant Height: 57-84 inches
Leaf Length: 20-22 inches
Leaf Width: 14-15 inches
Leaf Count: 20-26

Comments:

Yield:
Nicotine:

home-grown Corojo 99 puro

Photos: all RCAG

Cigar — Criollo (Cuba) — Cigar

Criollo (Cuba) was donated to ARS-GRIN by a refugee from Cuba in 1961, and was apparently one of Cuba's production cigar varieties at that time. It's growth and leaf closely resemble Coroja (Cuba). There is some variability in the maturation date, even within the same crop season and location. Air-cures easily. It can be primed or stalk-cut. A good variety for use as cigar wrapper, binder and filler.

ARS-GRIN incorrectly classifies this as an Oriental.

Days to Maturity: 45-60
Spacing: 24-36 inches
Plant Height: 43-46 inches
Leaf Length: 15-17½ inches
Leaf Width: 8-11 inches
Leaf Count: 15-17

Comments:

ARS-GRIN
PI 405646
Ti 1376
Yield: 2¼ ounces of cured leaf per plant
Nicotine: 3.41%

Photos: RCAG, ARS-GRIN, ARS-GRIN, RCAG

Cigar — Criollo 98 — Cigar

Criollo 98 is a Cuban cigar variety. It exhibits good productivity, and air-cures easily. It is useful for cigar wrapper, binder and filler. Resistant to the blue mold, some black shank and to Tobacco Mosaic Virus.

Days to Maturity: 84
Spacing: 24-36 inches
Plant Height: 52-72 inches
Leaf Length: 24 inches
Leaf Width: 12 inches
Leaf Count: 22-24

Comments:

Yield: ounces of cured leaf per plant
Nicotine:

Photos: Northwood Seeds, @Parequin

Cigar — Diamantina — Cigar

Diamantina is an heirloom cigar variety, collected from Diamantina, Minas Gerais, Brazil, by W.A. Archer, in 1936. Diamantina has a high nicotine content. The leaf's square venation pattern makes it suitable for cigar wrapper and binder. It provides an intense filler leaf.

Days to Maturity: 47-55
Spacing: 24-36 inches
Plant Height: 40½-48 inches
Leaf Length: 16-22 inches
Leaf Width: 8-12 inches
Leaf Count: 15-19

Comments:

ARS-GRIN
PI 118430
TI 959
Yield: 1½-2 ounces of cured leaf per plant
Nicotine: 5.9%

Photos: ARS-GRIN, ARS-GRIN, ARS-GRIN

Cigar — Dixie Shade — Cigar

Dixie Shade is a shade-grown cigar variety specifically for use as cigar wrapper. While it can be used as binder, its use as filler is minimal. Any low-grade leaf can be cooked into Cavendish, for a mild, pipe-blending ingredient. Growing Dixie Shade in full sun will yield coarser, smaller leaf.

Days to Maturity: 56-65
Spacing: 24-36 inches
Plant Height: 56-67 inches
Leaf Length: 18½-22 inches
Leaf Width: 11½-13½ inches
Leaf Count: 18-21

Pedigree
Date released: 1953. selected from root-knot resistant flue-cured variety RK 25 (developed from the cross TI 706/White Stem Orinoco//400)

Comments:

ARS-GRIN
PI 552353
TC 190
Yield: 2½-3 ounces of cured leaf per plant
Nicotine:

Photos: ARS-GRIN, ARS-GRIN, ARS-GRIN

Cigar — Florida 17 — Cigar

Florida 17 is a high yielding cigar wrapper variety which produces a quality leaf. It has a high level of resistance to black shank, is resistant to root knot nematodes, and tolerant of ozone-induced weather fleck. Florida 17 grows slowly early in the season but quickly catches up in the second half of the growing season. When grown in full sun the leaf will be thicker and more rugose than if grown in partial shade. Shade grown leaf will be flat, thinner and more elastic. It grows with little suckering. The light green leaves turn yellow at the edges and become mottled when ripe.

Days to Maturity: 76-84
Spacing: 24-36 inches
Plant Height: 71-77½ inches
Leaf Length: 16½-21½ inches
Leaf Width: 10½-14 inches
Leaf Count: 20-26

Pedigree:1970. No. 63/PD 42//2*Dixie Shade/3/2*No. 63/4/Connecticut B
Intellectual Property Rights
Crop Science Registration. CV-45, TOBACCO. Issued: 01 Nov 1970.

Comments:

ARS-GRIN
PI 552358
TC 192
Yield:
Nicotine:

Photos: ARS-GRIN, ARS-GRIN, ARS-GRIN

| Cigar | **Florida Sumatra** | Cigar |

Florida Sumatra is an heirloom tobacco that makes an excellent cigar wrapper when grown even in full sun (unlike Connecticut Shade varieties). Lower grade leaves serve well as binder, and make a mild filler ingredient.

Days to Maturity: 54-55
Spacing: 24-36 inches
Plant Height: 44½-52 inches
Leaf Length: 19-24 inches
Leaf Width: 11½-15 inches
Leaf Count: 18

Comments:

ARS-GRIN
PI 552631
TC 198
Yield: 2-2½ ounces of cured leaf per plant
Nicotine:

Home-grown Florida Sumatra Wrapper

Photos: RCAG, ARS-GRIN, RCAG, RCAG

Galickii

Cigar

Galickii is a Russian cigar tobacco suitable for use as a cigar wrapper, producing large, thin leaves. It air cures to a reddish brown. Galickii has its own interesting and individual aroma and taste.

Pedigree: (Pridnestrovskiy 5 x Temp)

Days to Maturity: 70-90
Spacing: 36 inches
Plant Height: 86-102 inches
Leaf Length: 24-28 inches
Leaf Width: 16-18 inches
Leaf Count: 26-30

Comments:

Yield: 1½-2 ounces of cured leaf per plant
Nicotine: 1.3%

Photos: Northwood Seeds, @madhouse

Cigar — Glessnor — Cigar

Glessnor (also spelled "Glessner") is an heirloom, Pennsylvania Seed Leaf variety from Lancaster County. It makes excellent cigar wrapper, binder and filler. Usually stalk-cut and air-cured on the stalk. It tends to color-cure to a deep, chestnut brown.

Days to Maturity: 53-59
Spacing: 24-36 inches
Plant Height: 36-39 inches
Leaf Length: 21-30 inches
Leaf Width: 7½-13 inches
Leaf Count: 14-19

Comments:

ARS-GRIN
PI 552642
TC 109
Yield: ~2 ounces of cured leaf per plant
Nicotine:

Photos: ARS-GRIN, RCAG, RCAG

Cigar — Habano 2000 — Cigar

Habano 2000 is a recently developed cigar variety, created specifically for wrapper. Sun grown plants are often used as a binder or filler. Grown under a shade cloth, Habano 2000 makes an excellent wrapper. Resistant to gray mold.

Pedigree: (Corojo x Cuban dark tobacco x Habano 2.1.1)

Days to Maturity:
Spacing: 24-36 inches
Plant Height: 72 inches
Leaf Length: 16 inches
Leaf Width: 9-10 inches
Leaf Count: 14-16

Comments:

Yield:
Nicotine:

Photos: Northwood Seeds

Hacienda del Cura

Hacienda del Cura is a Vuelta Abajo type of Cuban cigar tobacco that was grown in La Palma for many decades. Soon after the US embargo on Cuba, Canary Island cigars filled US consumer demand, until Cuban tobacco growing in Central America captured most of that market. The Hacienda del Cura leaf closely resembles the aroma and taste of Vuelta Abajo leaf, and can be used for wrapper, binder and filler.

Today, in the Canary Island of La Palma, there is no longer the Hacienda del Cura (mansion of the Priest), though there is a steep mountain road called *Calle de Hacienda del Cura*. This variety of tobacco was grown in that area until about 1982. Commercial production ended due to blue mold, to which the variety is sensitive.

Home-grown Hacienda del Cura puro.

Days to Maturity: 70
Spacing: 24-36 inches
Plant Height: 65-66 inches
Leaf Length: 17 inches
Leaf Width: 9 inches
Leaf Count: 19

Comments:

Yield:
Nicotine:

Photos: all RCAG

Cigar — Havana 142 — Cigar

Havana 142 was first developed in 1916 as cigar leaf. ARS-GRIN classifies it as a cigar binder, but it is often used in making chew. Many growers find it makes an excellent cigarette tobacco, as well as a mild blend component for pipe tobacco. A good choice for areas with short growing seasons. Air cures to a light brown. Resistant to black root rot.

Days to Maturity: 43-55
Spacing: 24-36 inches
Plant Height: 39-48 inches
Leaf Length: 20½-24½ inches
Leaf Width: 12 inches
Leaf Count: 17

Pedigree: 1923. Havana 38/Page's Comstock

Intellectual Property Rights
Crop Science Registration. CV-2, TOBACCO. Issued: 01 Nov 1958.

Comments:

ARS-GRIN
PI 552347
TC 91
Yield: 2½ ounces of cured leaf per plant
Nicotine:

Photos: ARS-GRIN, ARS-GRIN, ARS-GRIN

| Cigar | Havana 263 | Cigar |

Havana 263 is a cigar variety developed in Wisconsin, and classed as binder. It serves well as cigar wrapper, binder or filler. It air-cures easily, can be primed or stalk-cut. Cures to a light brown, sturdy leaf.

Days to Maturity: 55-59
Spacing: 24-36 inches
Plant Height: 34-47½ inches
Leaf Length: 20-25 inches
Leaf Width: 11-13 inches
Leaf Count: 20-22

Comments:

ARS-GRIN
PI 552434
TC 93
Yield: 3½-4 ounces of cured leaf per plant
Nicotine:

Photos: ARS-GRIN, ARS-GRIN, RCAG

Cigar   **Havana 322**   **Cigar**

Havana 322 is a cigar variety developed in Wisconsin. Though classed as binder, it is wonderful as wrapper, binder and filler. It is usually primed. It cures to a medium brown.

Black root rot resistant.

Pedigree: Havana 142/Havana 38

Days to Maturity: 48-90
Spacing: 24-36 inches
Plant Height: 42½-54 inches
Leaf Length: 23-26 inches
Leaf Width: 12½-14 inches
Leaf Count: 15-22

Home-grown Havana 322: viso (left) and seco.

Comments:

ARS-GRIN
PI 552435
TC 95
Yield: 2½ ounces of cured leaf per plant
Nicotine:

Photos: RCAG, ARS-GRIN, RCAG

| Cigar | Havana 38 | Cigar |

Havana 38 (also known as Wisconsin 38) is a cigar variety developed by the University of Wisconsin Ag. Experiment Station, and released in 1916. It can be used as cigar wrapper, binder and filler. It has a broader leaf, and is hardier than Havana 263. Air-cures to a medium brown.

Days to Maturity: 50-51
Spacing: 24-36 inches
Plant Height: 36-47 inches
Leaf Length: 19½-25 inches
Leaf Width: 10½-13 inches
Leaf Count: 17-19

Comments:

ARS-GRIN
PI 552432
TC 90
Yield: 2½ ounces of cured leaf per plant
Nicotine:

Photos: RCAG, ARS-GRIN, RCAG

Cigar — Havana 608 — Cigar

Havana 608 is a cigar filler or binder tobacco. The leaves are bright green, upturned, and with slightly down-turned tips. It holds up well during inclement weather and the pyramidal shape gives it good wind resistance. Air cures to a medium brown.

Days to Maturity: 65
Spacing: 24-36 inches
Plant Height: 42-72 inches
Leaf Length: 19-20 inches
Leaf Width: 12-16 inches
Leaf Count: 20

Comments:

Yield:
Nicotine:

Photos: Northwood Seeds, Northwood Seeds

Cigar   **Havana K2**   **Cigar**

Havana K2 is an early maturing variety classified as a cigar binder. It can be used as wrapper, binder or filler. Resistant to black root rot.

Days to Maturity: 48-50
Spacing: 24-36 inches
Plant Height: 44-46 inches
Leaf Length: 19-26 inches
Leaf Width: 12-15 inches
Leaf Count: 15-20

Pedigree: Havana Sandman/Havana 211//Havana Sandman

Comments:

ARS-GRIN
PI 552655
TC 102
Yield: 3 ounces of cured leaf per plant
Nicotine:

Photos: Northwood Seeds, ARS-GRIN, ARS-GRIN

Cigar   Havana K2-24   Cigar

Havana K2-24 is an early maturing variety classified as a cigar binder. It can be used for wrapper, binder and filler. Havana K2-24 has fewer suckers than Havana K2.

Days to Maturity: 48-52
Spacing: 24-36 inches
Plant Height: 44½-52 inches
Leaf Length: 20-23 inches
Leaf Width: 12-14 inches
Leaf Count: 17-18

Comments:

ARS-GRIN
PI 552656
TC 103
Yield: 3 ounces of cured leaf per plant
Nicotine:

Photos: Northwood Seeds, ARS-GRIN

Cigar — Havana Z992 — Cigar

Havana Z992 is a tall growing cigar variety, with good uniformity, and has little to no suckering before topping. The light green leaves turn yellow as soon as blooming begins and ripen soon after. This is a light colored, early-to-mid season Havana type. The leaves air-cure to a light brown. The variety was developed in Germany.

Days to Maturity: 55-90
Spacing: 24-36 inches
Plant Height: 60-72 inches
Leaf Length: 20 inches
Leaf Width: 12-14 inches
Leaf Count: 22-24

Comments:

Yield:
Nicotine:

Photos: Northwood Seeds, Northwood Seeds

Cigar — Jalapa — Cigar

Jalapa, classed as a cigar filler, is ideal for adding a rich flavor component. The Jalapa variety (received by ARS-GRIN in 1936, from Nicaragua) was grown near Nicaragua's border with Honduras, near the city of Jalapa. Its relatively narrow leaves and acute secondary vein angle render it a challenge for use as binder or wrapper. Its greatest drawback is a greater susceptibility to brown spot (*Alternaria alternata*) than many other tobacco varieties. Jalapa color-cures to a deep brown.

Days to Maturity: 38-55
Spacing: 24-36 inches
Plant Height: 45-58 inches
Leaf Length: 12-20½ inches
Leaf Width: 6-11½ inches
Leaf Count: 13-20

Concentric circles of brown spot (*Alternaria alternata*)

Comments:

ARS-GRIN
PI 114315
TI 615
Yield: 2½-5½ ounces of cured leaf per plant
Nicotine: 1.67%

Photos: ARS-GRIN, ARS-GRIN, RCAG, RCAG

Cigar   **Jamaica Wrapper**   **Cigar**

Jamaica Wrapper is classed by ARS-GRIN as a flue-cured variety, but has been used in the past as a blond cigar wrapper and plug wrapper.

Days to Maturity: 50-58
Spacing: 24-36 inches
Plant Height: 45½-49 inches
Leaf Length: 23½-25 inches
Leaf Width: 9½-12 inches
Leaf Count: 18

Comments:

ARS-GRIN
PI 552316
TC 317
Yield: 2-2½ ounces of cured leaf per plant
Nicotine:

Photos: ARS-GRIN, ARS-GRIN, RCAG

Kanburi

Cigar

Kanburi is a cigar filler variety that originated in Thailand. It can be planted with less spacing than most tobaccos at 18 inches.

Days to Maturity: 47-69
Spacing: 18-24 inches
Plant Height: 48½-56 inches
Leaf Length: 16-22 inches
Leaf Width: 7-10 inches
Leaf Count: 15-20

Comments:

ARS-GRIN
PI 405650
TI 1392
Yield: 1-2 ounces of cured leaf per plant
Nicotine: 3.13%

Photos: ARS-GRIN, ARS-GRIN, ARS-GRIN

| Cigar | L'Assomption 201 | Cigar |

L'Assomption 201 is a cigar filler variety developed in Canada, at the L'Assomption Experimental Station during the 1930s. It is useful for cigar wrapper, binder and filler. It air-cures easily to a deep, medium brown. It can be primed or stalk-cut and stalk-cured.

Days to Maturity: 51-52
Spacing: 24-36 inches
Plant Height: 43-44 inches
Leaf Length: 19-23½ inches
Leaf Width: 11-13 inches
Leaf Count: 18-19

Comments:

ARS-GRIN
PI 430516
TI 1624
Yield: 2-3 ounces of cured leaf per plant
Nicotine:

Photos: RCAG, Northwood Seeds, RCAG

Cigar — Lancaster Seed Leaf — Cigar

Lancaster Seed Leaf, grown extensively around Lancaster, Pennsylvania, is classified by ARS-GRIN as cigar filler, but its large leaves make it a good binder or wrapper as well. Cures to a deep brown color. The upper leaf can produce excellent "Pennsylvania maduro," for pipe blending.

Days to Maturity: 55-60
Spacing: 24-36 inches
Plant Height: 37-60 inches
Leaf Length: 19-29 inches
Leaf Width: 11-12½ inches
Leaf Count: 17-19

Comments:

ARS-GRIN
PI 552689
TC 113
Yield: 3 ounces of cured leaf per plant
Nicotine:

Photos: ARS-GRIN, ARS-GRIN, RCAG

Cigar — Little Dutch — Cigar

Little Dutch is an heirloom variety, released prior to 1883. It is sweet, aromatic tobacco used in pipe blends and as a cigar filler. The long narrow leaves also make an excellent cigar wrapper, but only for very thin cigars (stogies). Its low profile makes it a good choice for container growing. (Little Dutch is a sturdy, stocky plant, mostly the result of its close spacing between leaf nodes.) The dried blossoms of Little Dutch are uniquely aromatic, and worth collecting—at least once, for blending as a pipe ingredient. Little Dutch is stalk-cut, and air-cures easily. Resistant to black root rot.

Pedigree: Farmer selection introduced in Miamisburg, Ohio (just east of Germantown!), from Germany.

Days to Maturity: 40-47
Spacing: 24-36 inches
Plant Height: 29-32 inches
Leaf Length: 21-31½ inches
Leaf Width: 8-11 inches
Leaf Count: 13-16

Little Dutch upper leaf puro stogie

Comments:

ARS-GRIN
PI 551282
TC 114
Yield: 2 ounces of cured leaf per plant
Nicotine:

Photos: RCAG, ARS-GRIN, RCAG, RCAG

Cigar — Long Red — Cigar

Long Red is a cigar variety that is a good producer of high quality leaf for use as wrapper, binder and filler. The plants are usually stalk-cut and stalk-cured in the shed. The leaves cure to a reddish brown color. Cured aroma is similar to Pennsylvania Red.

Days to Maturity: 52-74
Spacing: 24-36 inches
Plant Height: 37-47 inches
Leaf Length: 24-29 inches
Leaf Width: 9½-12 inches
Leaf Count: 16-29

Long Red tied hands, one hand per stalk

Comments:

ARS-GRIN
PI 552693
TC 117
Yield: 2½ ounces of cured leaf per plant
Nicotine:

Photos: ARS-GRIN, RCAG, RCAG, RCAG

Cigar   **Machu Picchu Havana**   **Cigar**

Machu Picchu Havana is a unique cigar variety collected in Peru. In 1936, when Raymond Stadelman (Agricultural Explorer for the USDA) traveled to Machu Picchu by train, he was met at his destination by Carlos Duque, who had been the assistant of Hiram Bingham during the opening up of the Machu Picchu ruins in 1911-1915. There, he identified a tobacco said to have "white blossoms". The "white blossom" variety, found on Machu Picchu, was referred to by locals as "Havana". While ARS-GRIN still refers to this variety as "White Blossom", it should be called "Machu Picchu Havana" (c.f. the author). It is a wonderfully distinctive variant of Vuelta Abajo leaf, and produces maduro and oscuro cigar wrappers, excellent binders and flavorful filler. The blossoms are **pink**. (Later blossoms are occasionally nearly white.)

Pink blossom photographed at ARS-GRIN grow

Days to Maturity: 49-74
Spacing: 24-36 inches
Plant Height: 51-56 inches
Leaf Length: 20-21 inches
Leaf Width: 12½-13 inches
Leaf Count: 17-20

Home-grown Machu Picchu Havana puro

Comments:

ARS-GRIN
PI 116159
TI 719
Yield: 2-3½ ounces of cured leaf per plant
Nicotine: 4.06%

Photos: RCAG, ARS-GRIN, RCAG, RCAG

Magnolia

Cigar

Magnolia is a cigar wrapper which produces a high quality oval shaped leaf, and has little to no suckering before topping. Sun-grown, it yields a soft, medium-brown wrapper, and can also be used as binder. It offers minimal flavor when used as filler. Leaves should be primed. Shade-growing will significantly increase leaf size, and produce thinner wrapper.

Days to Maturity: 59-76
Spacing: 24-36 inches
Plant Height: 52-60 inches
Leaf Length: 16-21½ inches
Leaf Width: 10-12½ inches
Leaf Count: 24-31

Comments:

ARS-GRIN
PI 552354
TC 210
Yield: 2½ ounces of cured leaf per plant
Nicotine:

Photos: Northwood Seeds, ARS-GRIN, RCAG

Cigar   **Manila Wrapper**   **Cigar**

Manila Wrapper (misspelled in ARS-GRIN as "Manilla") cures to a relatively thin, medium brown wrapper leaf with square venation, and the mild flavor associated with Philippine cigar wrapper.

Days to Maturity: 47-65
Spacing: 24-36 inches
Plant Height: 53-67 inches
Leaf Length: 20-25 inches
Leaf Width: 10-12 inches
Leaf Count: 15-20

Comments:

ARS-GRIN
PI 404952
TI 78
Yield: 3½ ounces of cured leaf per plant
Nicotine: 2.96%

Photos: ARS-GRIN, ARS-GRIN, ARS-GRIN

Cigar — Matsukawa — Cigar

Matsukawa is a cigar filler from Japan (donated to ARS-GRIN in 1935). Because of the acute angle of secondary veins, it is not as useful as wrapper or binder, though it can be used as such when rolling narrower cigars.

Days to Maturity: 43-60
Spacing: 24-36 inches
Plant Height: 32-35½ inches
Leaf Length: 21-23 inches
Leaf Width: 12-16 inches
Leaf Count: 16

Comments:

ARS-GRIN
PI 405005
TI 168
Yield: 2-3½ ounces of cured leaf per plant
Nicotine: 3.95%

Photos: ARS-GRIN, ARS-GRIN, ARS-GRIN

Cigar — Matsukawa Kanto 201 — Cigar

Matsukawa Kanto 201 is a cigar filler from Japan. It is unusual for a cigar variety, in that it is a columnar plant with a heart-shaped leaf that grows on a petiole (bare leaf stem) Flower is nearly pure white. It's acute angle of secondary veins renders it difficult to use as a wrapper or binder.

Days to Maturity: 55-73
Spacing: 24-36 inches
Plant Height: 48-60 inches
Leaf Length: 20-26 inches
Leaf Width: 11-16 inches
Leaf Count: 20-24

Comments:

ARS-GRIN
PI 390127
TI 1588

Yield: 3-4 ounces of cured leaf per plant
Nicotine: 4.14%

Photos: ARS-GRIN, Northwood Seeds, ARS-GRIN

Metacomet

Cigar

Metacomet is a cigar wrapper developed in Connecticut. It is intended to be shade-grown. When sun-grown, the leaf is smaller and thicker, but still makes a presentable wrapper or binder. Leaf should be primed.

Resistance to the tobacco cyst nematode (*Globodera tabacum*) and TMV.

Days to Maturity: 70
Spacing: 24-36 inches
Plant Height: 76-92 inches
Leaf Length: 15 inches
Leaf Width: 10 inches
Leaf Count: 33

Pedigree: 1999. 0-30/VA 81

Intellectual Property Rights
Crop Science Registration. CV-120, TOBACCO. Issued: 01 Sep 2000.

Comments:

ARS-GRIN
PI 612391
TC 652
Yield:
Nicotine:

Photos: ARS-GRIN, ARS-GRIN, RCAG

Mont-Calme Brun

Cigar

Mont-Calme Brun (Brown) is a cigar wrapper variety from Switzerland. (Sota Experiment Station, Nyon) 1970. It is low in nicotine, and rather mild in taste and aroma. Resistant to black rot and PVYn.

Days to Maturity: 58-65
Spacing: 24-36 inches
Plant Height: 47 inches
Leaf Length: 17-23 inches
Leaf Width: 9½-14 inches
Leaf Count: 15-23

Comments:

ARS-GRIN
PI 355071
TI 1505
Yield: 2-3½ ounces of cured leaf per plant
Nicotine: 1.17%

Photos: ARS-GRIN, ARS-GRIN, RCAG

Cigar — Moonlight — Cigar

Moonlight is a cigar wrapper which produces a thin, smoothly flavored wrapper. Even when sun-grown, its leaves are larger and thinner than sun-grown Florida Sumatra. Suckers are nearly absent before topping. Moonlight is similar to Magnolia.

Days to Maturity: 65-76
Spacing: 24-36 inches
Plant Height: 62½-72 inches
Leaf Length:18-22 inches
Leaf Width: 11½-14 inches
Leaf Count: 18-27

Comments:

ARS-GRIN
PI 552702
TC 211
Yield: 2½ ounces of cured leaf per plant
Nicotine:

Photos: Northwood Seeds, ARS-GRIN, RCAG

Cigar — Nacional — Cigar

Nacional is an heirloom cigar tobacco dating back to 1935, from Montevideo, Uruguay. ARS-GRIN market class is "other." The leaf generally resembles Paraguay Flojo, and may be a variation of that high Andes type.

Days to Maturity: 54-68
Spacing: 24-36 inches
Plant Height: 41-61½ inches
Leaf Length: 21-24½ inches
Leaf Width: 10-12 inches
Leaf Count: 14-25

Comments:

ARS-GRIN
PI 112705
TI 368
Yield: 1¼-3½ ounces of cured leaf per plant
Nicotine: 1.25%

Photos: ARS-GRIN, ARS-GRIN, ARS-GRIN

Native 10 (Bolivia)

Cigar | **Cigar**

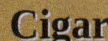

Native 10 is an heirloom cigar filler from Bolivia. (Acquired by ARS-GRIN in 1956.) Suckering is low.

Days to Maturity: 49-68
Spacing: 24-36 inches
Plant Height: 49-53½ inches
Leaf Length: 21-24 inches
Leaf Width: 8-13½ inches
Leaf Count: 13-22

Comments:

ARS-GRIN
PI 235562
TI 1303
Yield: 2½-3 ounces of cured leaf per plant
Nicotine: 3.57%

Photos: ARS-GRIN, ARS-GRIN, ARS-GRIN

Cigar — **No. 3666 Deli** — **Cigar**

No. 3666 Deli (ARS-GRIN classed as "primitive") is said to have been originally smuggled out of Sumatra to Honduras, and is said to be a pure strain of the best type grown in Sumatra. [Collected by W. A. Archer, 1936.] Sumatra Deli is primarily used as cigar wrapper. The provenance of this particular seed is unclear.

Days to Maturity: 37-46
Spacing: 24-36 inches
Plant Height: 79-84 inches
Leaf Length: 13-17 inches
Leaf Width: 5½-8½ inches
Leaf Count: 11-15

Comments:

ARS-GRIN
PI 113718
TI 489
Yield: 1-1½ ounces of cured leaf per plant
Nicotine: 4.92%

Photos: ARS-GRIN, ARS-GRIN, ARS-GRIN

Nostrano del Brenta

Cigar | **Cigar**

Nostrano del Brenta is a remarkable, heirloom cigar wrapper variety from the Brenta valley of northern Italy. The plant is a vigorous grower that produces large leaves, often color-curing to deep maduro or oscuro wrappers, both with a mild taste and aroma. There is an Italian commercial cigar named, "Nostrano del Brenta," made from this variety.

[Shortly after the first journey of Columbus to the New World (during the 1500s), tobacco was introduced into the Brenta River Valley of Italy. This variety may be considered a landrace that has been relatively stable for over 500 years.]

There were 3 sub-varieties: Cuchetto, Avanino (little Havana) and Avanone (Campesano). All three of these were lost forever during the 1960s. Only a hybrid variant, known specifically as "Nostrano Gentile" is still cultivated. This is that variety.

Home-grown Nostrano del Brenta lower leaf.

Home-grown Nostrano del Brenta mid leaf.

Home-grown Nostrano del Brenta top leaf.

Days to Maturity: 62
Spacing: 24-36 inches
Plant Height: 47-51 inches
Leaf Length: 24 inches
Leaf Width: 19 inches
Leaf Count: 18

Comments:

Yield:
Nicotine:

Photos: All RCAG

Cigar   **Ohio Dutch**   **Cigar**

Ohio Dutch is classed as cigar filler, but also makes beautiful wrappers and sturdy binders. Its flavor is similar to that of Little Dutch, though softer, and Ohio Dutch leaves are larger.

[For unknown reasons, ARS-GRIN has removed any reference to "Ohio" for this accession. Prior to their database renovation, the name was listed as "Dutch (Ohio)".]

Days to Maturity: 50-65
Spacing: 24-36 inches
Plant Height: 40-56 inches
Leaf Length: 21-30 inches
Leaf Width: 8-11½ inches
Leaf Count: 15-23

Comments:

ARS-GRIN
PI 552627
TC 107
Yield: 2-2½ ounces of cured leaf per plant
Nicotine:

Photos: RCAG, ARS-GRIN, RCAG

Cigar — Olor (Dominican Republic) — Cigar

Olor (Dominican Republic) is a cigar wrapper variety that produces the distinctive taste and aroma of many Dominican cigars. It's intense, dark aromas are excellent in filler blending, and the sturdy leaf serves well as a binder. *[The ARS-GRIN name of this variety is "Cigar Wrapper (Dom. Rep)."]* Olor can be stalk-harvested and cured on the stalk.

Days to Maturity: 60-63
Spacing: 24-36 inches
Plant Height: 54-72 inches
Leaf Length: 21-25 inches
Leaf Width: 9-14 inches
Leaf Count: 19-22

Home-grown Olor (Dominican) oscuro wrapper

Comments:

ARS-GRIN
PI 552617
TC 182
Yield: 3 ounces of cured leaf per plant
Nicotine:

Photos: RCAG, ARS-GRIN, RCAG, RCAG

Cigar — Pennsylvania Red — Cigar

Pennsylvania Red is a cigar variety, once used commonly for US-style cigar filler. For narrow cigars, it can serve well as binder or wrapper. It's flavor and aroma are a bit more intense than that of Long Red, but the PA Red is somewhat less productive. Leaves air-cure to a deep reddish brown.

Days to Maturity: 58-70
Spacing: 24-36 inches
Plant Height: 36-48½ inches
Leaf Length: 21½-29 inches
Leaf Width: 9-11 inches
Leaf Count: 15-25

Comments:

ARS-GRIN
PI 552741
TC 124
Yield: 2 ounces of cured leaf per plant
Nicotine:

Photos: RCAG, ARS-GRIN, RCAG

Cigar — Pergeu — Cigar

Pergeu is a dark air-cure tobacco that originated in Brazil. It is primarily used in Europe for cigar filler tobacco, as well as for pipe and cigarette blending. It produces a large, thick, heavy-weight leaf. Resistant to blue mold. Air cures to a deep rich brown color. The lower lugs (leaves 4 thru 8 from the bottom) are sometimes selected as cigar wrapper.

Days to Maturity: 55-60
Spacing: 24-36 inches
Plant Height: 60 inches
Leaf Length: 15-18 inches
Leaf Width: ~7 inches
Leaf Count: 14-16

Comments:

Yield:
Nicotine:

Photos: Northwood Seeds, Northwood Seeds, Northwood Seeds

Cigar — Piloto Cubano (Puerto Rico) — Cigar

Piloto Cubano (Puerto Rico) is a traditional, Dominican Piloto Cubano cigar tobacco that was sourced from a start-up tobacco plantation in Puerto Rico. Piloto Cubano means, "Cuban seed", but dates back to the days of the early 20th century, when Cuban-grown tobacco was a mix of assorted, unknown variants—and prior to recognition of Mendelian genetics, with its implications for maintaining seed purity. Piloto Cubano is a full-bodied cigar variety that is used primarily in filler blends, to broaden the flavor and add strength. It can, of course, make striking wrappers and sturdy binders.

Days to Maturity: 56-73
Spacing: 24-36 inches
Plant Height: 63 inches
Leaf Length: 24 inches
Leaf Width: 14 inches
Leaf Count: 18-20

Home-grown Piloto Cubano (Puerto Rico) wrappers: lower leaf and upper leaf (dark)

Comments:

Yield:
Nicotine:

Photos: all RCAG

Piloto Cubano PR Broad

Cigar | **Cigar**

Piloto Cubano PR Broad is a Piloto Cubano cigar tobacco that began as Piloto Cubano (Puerto Rico), and was subsequently grower-selected for consistent height and consistently broad leaf. The result is a Piloto Cubano that is more productive. Piloto Cubano is a full-bodied cigar variety that is used primarily in filler blends, to broaden the flavor and add strength. It can make striking wrappers and sturdy binders.

Days to Maturity: 56-73
Spacing: 24-36 inches
Plant Height: 72-96 inches
Leaf Length: 27 inches
Leaf Width: 12-14 inches
Leaf Count: 18-26

Comments:

Yield:
Nicotine:

Photos: RCAG, RCAG

Cigar — Punta De Lanza — Cigar

Punta De Lanza is a cigar filler from Zacapa, Guatemala, collected by W.A. Archer in 1936. Its square venation pattern is compatible with use as wrapper or binder, but Punta De Lanza has a very high nicotine content.

Days to Maturity: 45-65
Spacing: 24-36 inches
Plant Height: 42-44 inches
Leaf Length: 15-18½ inches
Leaf Width: 8-11 inches
Leaf Count: 16-18

Comments:

ARS-GRIN
PI 113590
TI 464
Yield: ½-2 ounces of cured leaf per plant
Nicotine: 6.44%

Photos: ARS-GRIN, ARS-GRIN

Red Rose

Cigar / **Cigar**

Red Rose is a Pennsylvania cigar filler variety that can be used as wrapper and binder as well. The leaf tends to be large and thick. Air-cures to a deep brown.

Days to Maturity: 44-64
Spacing: 24-36 inches
Plant Height: 35½-39 inches
Leaf Length: 23-26 inches
Leaf Width: 11½-12 inches
Leaf Count: 15-25

Comments:

ARS-GRIN
PI 552357
TC 130
Yield: 2½-3 ounces of cured leaf per plant
Nicotine:

Photos: ARS-GRIN, ARS-GRIN, RCAG

Cigar — San Andrés — Cigar

San Andrés is a cigar variety collected in Mexico, in 1929. "A special variety said to be from the best tobacco grown in the vicinity of San Andres Tuxtla." Classed by USDA as a cigar filler, the leaf makes excellent wrappers and binders.

[The distinctive, lightly smoky aroma of commercial San Andrés leaf is created by heating the curing barns with low fires of dried banana plant debris.]

Days to Maturity: 45-70
Spacing: 24-36 inches
Plant Height: 50-60 inches
Leaf Length: 17-22 inches
Leaf Width: 9-12 inches
Leaf Count: 17-21

Comments:

ARS-GRIN
PI 80250
TI 117
Yield: 2-3 ounces of cured leaf per plant
Nicotine: 3.17%

Photos: ARS-GRIN, ARS-GRIN, RCAG

Cigar — Suifu — Cigar

Suifu is an heirloom cigar wrapper from Japan which was received by ARS-GRIN in 1935. The leaves are unusual for cigar varieties, in that they are petiolate (bare leaf stem). Their square venation pattern is an advantage in making wrappers and binders. The nicotine level is high.

Days to Maturity: 42-63
Spacing: 24-36 inches
Plant Height: 44½-52 inches
Leaf Length: 18-20 inches
Leaf Width: 9½-11 inches
Leaf Count: 13-20

Comments:

ARS-GRIN
PI 405004
TI 167
Yield: 2-2½ ounces of cured leaf per plant
Nicotine: 5.34%

Photos: ARS-GRIN, ARS-GRIN

Cigar   **Swarr-Hibshman**   **Cigar**

Swarr-Hibshman is a Pennsylvania seedleaf variety classed as cigar filler. ARS-GRIN lists three different Swarr-Hibshman accessions, as well as the earlier "Swarr," all from Pennsylvania. Any of these will give roughly similar results. The variety is productive of large, thick leaf, useful for cigar wrapper, binder and filler, as well as pipe blending.

Days to Maturity: 50-70
Spacing: 24-36 inches
Plant Height: 39-52 inches
Leaf Length: 21-29½ inches
Leaf Width: 14 inches
Leaf Count: 14-23

Comments:

ARS-GRIN ("Pennsylvania Swarr-Hibshman")
PI 552733
TC 120
Yield: 2-3 ounces of cured leaf per plant
Nicotine:

Photos: RCAG, ARS-GRIN, RCAG

Cigar — Timor — Cigar

Timor is a cigar wrapper variety that was grown in Java, Indonesia in 1956. The leaf is a slightly thicker leaf than "Sumatra" Deli leaf as well as Besuki, but is still reasonably thin when grown in full-sun. It makes good cigar wrapper, binder and filler. Flavor and aroma are similar to Sumatra and Besuki leaf.

Days to Maturity: 51-81
Spacing: 24-36 inches
Plant Height: 53½-76 inches
Leaf Length: 18-20 inches
Leaf Width: 9-12 inches
Leaf Count: 18-30

Home-grown Timor wrapper.

Comments:

ARS-GRIN
PI 405659
TI 1402
Yield: 2-3 ounces of cured leaf per plant
Nicotine: 2.89%

Photos: RCAG, ARS-GRIN, RCAG, RCAG

Cigar — Uruguay — Cigar

Uruguay is a cigar filler. Its square venation pattern makes it also useful as cigar wrapper and binder.

Days to Maturity: 45-85
Spacing: 24-36 inches
Plant Height: 37½-60 inches
Leaf Length: 17-24 inches
Leaf Width: 9½-12 inches
Leaf Count: 14-20

Comments:

ARS-GRIN
PI 404938
TI 25
Yield: 1½-3 ounces of cured leaf per plant
Nicotine: 1.91%

Photos: ARS-GRIN, ARS-GRIN, ARS-GRIN

Cigar — Vallejano — Cigar

Vallejano is an heirloom cigar filler from Mexico. Vallejano has a high nicotine content. It was collected by W.A. Archer from Puerto Vallarta, Jalisco, in 1935.

"This variety is said to have originated at Valle Banderas, a place near Campostela (Nayarit). The leaf is said to have naked petiole and was one of the most important varieties before the introduction of American types." *[This variety produces a sessile leaf attachment, rather than a bare petiole (leaf stem).]*

Days to Maturity: 40-50
Spacing: 24-36 inches
Plant Height: 31½-36 inches
Leaf Length: 21-24 inches
Leaf Width: 9-12 inches
Leaf Count: 14-16

Comments:

ARS-GRIN
PI 112183
TI 216
Yield: 2-2½ ounces of cured leaf per plant
Nicotine: 5.92%

Photos: Northwood Seeds, ARS-GRIN

Cigar — Vuelta Abajo — Cigar

Vuelta Abajo is an heirloom cigar variety from Cuba's famed, Vuelta Abajo region. It is an ancestor to the later, Criollo and Corojo varieties, and is likely the original source of Peru's Machu Picchu Havana. The leaves are excellent for use as cigar wrappers. Its rich aroma and full body are ideal for cigar filler. While not as productive as Corojo 99 and Criollo 98, this cigar variety is an excellent choice for home growers. Its upper leaf produces deep oscuro leaf.

[ARS-GRIN mis-classifies this as "Oriental."]

Days to Maturity: 43-54
Spacing: 24-36 inches
Plant Height: 40-60 inches
Leaf Length: 12-16 inches
Leaf Width: 7-12 inches
Leaf Count: 11-16

Home-grown Vuelta Abajo wrappers.

Comments:

ARS-GRIN
PI 405668
TI 1453
Yield: 1½-2 ounces of cured leaf per plant
Nicotine: 4.6%

Photos: RCAG, ARS-GRIN, RCAG, RCAG, RCAG

Cigar — Wisconsin 901 — Cigar

Wisconsin 901 is classed as a cigar binder but may be used as a wrapper or filler. It produces large leaves, has a tight, upright form. Tensile strength is good. Relatively mild flavor and aroma.

Days to Maturity: 55-60
Spacing: 24-36 inches
Plant Height: 48-49 inches
Leaf Length: 22 inches
Leaf Width: 9½ inches
Leaf Count: 21

Comments:

Yield:
Nicotine:

Photos: Northwood Seeds, RCAG

Cigar **Wisconsin Seedleaf** **Cigar**

Wisconsin Seedleaf is classed as cigar binder, though it produces generously sized leaves that make wonderful wrappers and medium-bodied filler. The variety was donated by the University of Wisconsin in 1963. It can be stalk-cut, and air-cured on the stalk.

Days to Maturity: 46-53
Spacing: 24-36 inches
Plant Height: 36-40½ inches
Leaf Length: 21-25 inches
Leaf Width: 14-16 inches
Leaf Count: 16-18

Comments:

ARS-GRIN
PI 552436
TC 106
Yield: 2-2½ ounces of cured leaf per plant
Nicotine:

Photos: ARS-GRIN, ARS-GRIN, RCAG

Zimmer Spanish

Cigar | **Cigar**

Zimmer Spanish is an heirloom cigar filler, released prior to 1905. *"Leaves are medium in size, have good body and elasticity with small veins, and they resemble the Cuban variety."* [That is fanciful imagery from the early days of GRIN.] It is most likely a combination of a seedleaf variety with an unknown, Cuban variety. Pre-1905 means no understanding of how adjacently planted tobacco varieties hybridize. Zimmer Spanish is a fortunate accident. Suckering is low.

Days to Maturity: 45-50
Spacing: 24-36 inches
Plant Height: 32-48 inches
Leaf Length: 18-22 inches
Leaf Width: 10-12 inches
Leaf Count: 14-20

Comments:

ARS-GRIN
PI 551284
TC 136
Yield: 1½-2 ounces of cured leaf per plant
Nicotine:

Photos: ARS-GRIN, ARS-GRIN, RCAG

Dark   **Adonis**   **Dark**

Adonis is a dark air-cured variety grown in Germany. It is said to have "very low nicotine content, yet spicy flavor characteristics."* This vigorous early season grower performs very well in cooler climates producing a dark green, heavy-weight leaf. It has closely spaced leaves. Its low dense growth makes it more resistant to adverse weather conditions. Mature plants have some frost resistance.

*tabakanbau.de

Days to Maturity: ?? "early season"
Spacing: 24-36 inches
Plant Height: 60 inches
Leaf Length: 18 inches
Leaf Width: 12 inches
Leaf Count: 14-16

Comments:

Yield:
Nicotine:

Photos: Northwood Seeds, Northwood Seeds

Dark   Ainaro   Dark

Ainaro is a variety of Dark sun-cured leaf. It was collected from the tobacco garden of a simple home outside the town of Ainaro, by Anton Eise DeVries, during his exploration of Timor Leste in 2016. The most distinctive characteristic of its large leaves is their petiole (bare leaf stem), suggestive of some pre-WW2, Japanese cigar varieties. It can be stalk-cut, and sun-cured on the stalk, or primed. The finished leaf has a spicy character. It also cooks into a tasty Cavendish. Suitable for pipe blending.

Days to Maturity: 77
Spacing: 24-36 inches
Plant Height: 53-60 inches
Leaf Length: 22 inches
Leaf Width: 13 inches
Leaf Count: 18

Comments:

Yield:
Nicotine:

Tobacco growing near Ainaro

Photos: RCAG, RCAG, RCAG, Anton Eise deVries

Dark   **Bolivian Criollo Black**   **Dark**

Bolivian Criollo Black is not classified, but appears to be typical of many tobaccos from the Andes high plains, such as Paraguay Flojo. It is a vigorous grower and heavy producer. The leaves are very sticky. Its flavor is distinctive, with a terpene taste that eventually dissipates. The leaf can be used in cigars, pipe blends and as a minor component in cigarette blends. It can be made into oral tobacco.

["Bolivian Black is the common name for five varieties: Americano Extranjero, Palo Amarillo, Paraguayo 112, Paraguayo M1 and Rifarachi. We all grow the one of this varieties, but I don't know which of the five."]*

*@polygon55

Home-grown Bolivian Criollo Black wrapper.

Days to Maturity: 68-70
Spacing: 24-36 inches
Plant Height: 60-90 inches
Leaf Length: 20½-30 inches
Leaf Width: 8½-13 inches
Leaf Count: 24-28

Comments:

Yield:
Nicotine:

Photos: all RCAG

Dark   # Goose Creek Red   **Dark**

Goose Creek Red is a dark Virginia type tobacco that air-cures to a deep reddish brown color. It is useful for full-flavored pipe and cigarette blends. Said to have "a cigarette aroma."

Days to Maturity: 56-65
Spacing: 24-36 inches
Plant Height: 51-60 inches
Leaf Length: 18-25½ inches
Leaf Width: 6-9 inches
Leaf Count: 18-20

Comments:

ARS-GRIN
PI *none*
TC 644
Yield:
Nicotine:

Photos: ARS-GRIN, ARS-GRIN, ARS-GRN

Dark **Greenwood** **Dark**

Greenwood, also called Little Wood, is an heirloom fire-cured tobacco that has been used for chew, as cigar filler and wrapper, and as a blend component for cigarettes.

Days to Maturity: 52-67
Spacing: 24-36 inches
Plant Height: 40½-60 inches
Leaf Length: 24-25 inches
Leaf Width: 10½-14 inches
Leaf Count: 16-18

Comments:

ARS-GRIN
PI 552646
TC 469
Yield: 2½ ounces of cured leaf per plant
Nicotine:

Photos: ARS-GRIN, ARS-GRIN, ARS-GRIN

India Black **Dark**

India Black is a very dark cigar and pipe tobacco. The plant has the look of a Virginia-type tobacco. The large leaves are dark green, lightening and bending down as they ripen. Air-cures to a dark brown.

Days to Maturity: 60-65
Spacing: 24-36 inches
Plant Height: 48-60 inches
Leaf Length: 25 inches
Leaf Width: 12 inches
Leaf Count: 14-16

Comments:

Yield:
Nicotine:

Photos: Northwood Seeds, Northwood Seeds

Dark   **Liquiça**   **Dark**

Liquiça is a variety of Dark sun-cured leaf. It was collected from the tobacco garden of a home outside the town of Liquiça by Anton Eise DeVries, during his exploration of Timor Leste in 2016. Liquiça can be stalk-cut, and sun-cured on the stalk, or primed. It is traditionally cured using the ranjangan method of shredding the mature green leaf, then spreading it to sun-cure on basketry frames. The finished leaf is richly flavored. Suitable for pipe blending or in strong cigarettes.

Days to Maturity: 80-90
Spacing: 24-36 inches
Plant Height: 64 inches
Leaf Length: 18 inches
Leaf Width: 10 inches
Leaf Count: 24

Comments:

Yield:
Nicotine:

Photos: all RCAG

Little Yellow

Dark — **Dark**

Little Yellow is a truly unique, American heirloom, Dark air-cure tobacco, developed prior to 1900. Like other dark tobaccos, the leaves are thick and sticky (from bountiful leaf trichomes—leaf hairs), and its nicotine load is relatively high, though lower than many other dark varieties. It air-cures to a deep yellow-red, and offers a surprisingly smooth and distinctive flavor and aroma. It is good for making various oral tobacco preparations. It excels as a pipe blending ingredient, and also cooks into a richly flavored, smooth Cavendish. It can be a delightful substitute for any other dark air-cured ingredient in blending recipes.

Days to Maturity: 47-56
Spacing: 24-36 inches
Plant Height: 48 inches
Leaf Length: 25 inches
Leaf Width: 14 inches
Leaf Count: 14-20

Pedigree: Farmer selection

Comments:

ARS-GRIN
PI 551289
TC 222
Yield:
Nicotine: 3.53%

Photos: RCAG, ARS-GRIN, RCAG

Dark Madole Dark

Madole is an heirloom dark tobacco with a rich full flavor. It is often fire cured for use in a pipe blend or chew. It is also used in snuff recipes. Madole can be air-cured. It is usually stalk-cut.

["...dark tobacco is much later to harvest [than burley] and if you are growing it and are treating it like a burley, you will be priming incurable green leaf. My observation among [Little Yellow, Black Mammoth and Madole] is that Madole, hands down was the biggest and strongest producer."]*

*@Cray Squirrel

Days to Maturity: 52-57
Spacing: 24-36 inches
Plant Height: 45 inches
Leaf Length: 25-25½ inches
Leaf Width: 7-10½ inches
Leaf Count: 16-18

Comments:

ARS-GRIN
PI 552438
TC 479
Yield: 1½-2 ounces of cured leaf per plant
Nicotine:

Photos: Northwood Seeds, ARS-GRIN, ARS-GRIN

One Sucker

Dark | **Dark**

One Sucker is a *category* of dark tobaccos, but the name is applied to over a dozen specific varieties, which mostly differ from one another in disease resistance. It has variously been fire-cured and air-cured. ARS-GRIN lists only three varieties. Doug Moats of the Nicotiana Project listed twelve more. Most "One Sucker" varieties have suckering rates similar to those of other tobacco varieties. "One Sucker" was marketing hype at the turn of the 20th century. For most home growers, any available One Sucker variety will likely serve as well as any other.

Days to Maturity: 55-80
Spacing: 24-36 inches
Plant Height: 39-48 inches (waist to chest high)
Leaf Length: 23-30 inches
Leaf Width: 8-12 inches
Leaf Count: 14-20

Comments:
Three varieties listed by ARS-GRIN
a)PI 551290; b)PI 604199; c)PI 604198
a)TC 224; b)TC 639; c)TC 638
a)"One Sucker"; b)VA 359; c)VA 355

Yield: ~2 ounces of cured leaf per plant
Nicotine:

Photos: Northwood Seeds, ARS-GRIN (TC 638), ARS-GRIN (TC 638)

Dark   **Rot Front**   **Dark**

Rot Front (Red Front) is a dark air-cured variety. "The dark, air-dried Korso variety was grown in eastern Germany in Lusatia and is now mainly used as cigar tobacco in Austria, in the Oder region and in northern Baden."* It is also used in cigarette and pipe blends. It has a medium nicotine content and the flavor is sometimes described as spicy. It is a good producer. The leaves are closely space and upright.

*tabakanbau.de

Days to Maturity: 60
Spacing: 24-36 inches
Plant Height: 48-72 inches
Leaf Length: 20 inches
Leaf Width: 11-14 inches
Leaf Count: 18-20

Comments:

Yield:
Nicotine:

Photos: Northwood Seeds, Northwood Seeds

Tobacco Plant Varieties for Home Growers 181

| Dark | Shirey | Dark |

Shirey is a Dark Virginia variety of tobacco, useful for cigarette and pipe blending. It produces a large leaf that air-cures easily to a medium brown. It is a hardy plant that withstands moderate late season frosts.

Days to Maturity: 63-65
Spacing: 24-36 inches
Plant Height: 66 inches
Leaf Length: 20-25½ inches
Leaf Width: 6-9 inches
Leaf Count: 12-16

Comments:

ARS-GRIN
PI *none*
TC 617
Yield:
Nicotine:

Photos: Northwood Seeds, ARS-GRIN, ARS-GRIN

Dark — Small Stalk Black Mammoth — Dark

Small Stalk Black Mammoth is an heirloom Dark air-cured tobacco. It is useful for oral preparations, snuff tobacco and pipe blending. It also cooks into a full-bodied Cavendish. The leaves are sometimes fire-cured. It is stalk-cut.

Days to Maturity: 55-60
Spacing: 24-36 inches
Plant Height: 24-48 inches
Leaf Length: 30 inches
Leaf Width: 16 inches
Leaf Count: 14-18

Comments:

ARS-GRIN
PI *none*
TC 641
Yield:
Nicotine:

Photos: Northwood Seeds, Northwood Seeds

Dark **Staghorn** **Dark**

Staghorn is a hardy Dark air-cured Virginia that grows fast, with long, thick, narrow leaves. The leaves turn under at the tips, resembling a staghorn. It has a rich, full flavor and is good for cigarettes and pipe blending. The leaves air-cure to a deep reddish brown.

Days to Maturity: 65
Spacing: 24-36 inches
Plant Height: 64-72 inches
Leaf Length: 15-26 inches
Leaf Width: 6-16 inches
Leaf Count: 18-20

Comments:

Yield:
Nicotine:

Photos: Northwood Seeds, Northwood Seeds

Szamosi Dark

Szamosi Dark is an air-cured Hungarian variety. Its square venation pattern allows its use as a full-bodied cigar wrapper. It can be used in oral preparations, strong cigarette blends and pipe blending.

Days to Maturity: 55-60
Spacing: 24-36 inches
Plant Height: 60 inches
Leaf Length: 24-16 inches
Leaf Width: 12-14 inches
Leaf Count: 12-14

Comments:

Yield: 3-4 ounces of cured leaf per plant
Nicotine:

Photos: Northwood Seeds, Northwood Seeds

Tabaco Negro (Spain)

Dark

Tabaco Negro (Spain) is a name for a Dark tobacco that is dark in color and strong in taste. Black or dark tobacco is primarily used in cigars and dark cigarettes. It is often slowly darkened by a long curing and fermenting process to give a dark brown to black tobacco with exceptionally mild smoking characteristics.

Days to Maturity: 55-60
Spacing: 24-36 inches
Plant Height: 60-72 inches
Leaf Length: 20-22 inches
Leaf Width: 12-14 inches
Leaf Count: 14-16

Comments:

Yield:
Nicotine:

Photos: Northwood Seeds, Northwood Seeds

Dark — VA 355 — Dark

VA 355 is a Dark fire-cured tobacco variety developed at Virginia Tech. Fewer than one ground sucker per 18 plants. Average leaf length and width of both the middle and top leaf are the same. VA 355 can also be air-cured, for a richly flavored, potent blending ingredient in cigarette or pipe blending.

Resistant to race 0 black shank and more resistant to race 1 black shank than VA 309.

Days to Maturity: 59
Spacing: 36 inches
Plant Height: 23 inches to crowfoot
Leaf Length: 31 inches
Leaf Width: 14½ inches
Leaf Count: 12

Pedigree 1998: VA 309/VA 312//DF 300

Intellectual Property Rights
Crop Science Registration. CV-115, TOBACCO. Issued: 01 Jan 1999.

Comments:

ARS-GRIN
PI 604198
TC 638
Yield:
Nicotine: 5.59%

Home-grown, cured hand of VA 355

Photos: ARS-GRIN, ARS-GRIN, Wallace Kemp

Dark — Viqueque — Dark

Viqueque is a variety of Dark sun-cured leaf. It was collected from the tobacco garden of a home outside the town of Viqueque by Anton Eise DeVries, during his exploration of Timor Leste in 2016. Viqueque can be stalk-cut, and sun-cured on the stalk, or primed. It is traditionally cured using the ranjangan method of shredding the mature green leaf, then spreading it to sun-cure on basketry frames. The finished leaf is richly flavored. Suitable for pipe blending or in strong cigarettes.

"The Viqueque air cured is no different from the Delhi 34 air cured. It flue cured poorly. The sun cured is really good, like a Virginia with no bite. The fire cured is versatile. It blends well with everything. It also gives nice flavour to a cigar when used as binder without tasting acidic."*

*Stewart Cranston

Days to Maturity: ?
Spacing: 24-36 inches
Plant Height: 48-60 inches
Leaf Length: 23-26 inches
Leaf Width: 12-14 inches
Leaf Count: 14-18

Comments:

Yield:
Nicotine:

Photos: Anton Eise deVries, Stewart Cranston

Dark   **Walker's Broadleaf**   **Dark**

Walker's Broadleaf is an improved Fire-cure variety donated in 1961 by the Virginia Crop Improvement Association. It can also be air-cured. Useful for oral tobacco and as a flavorant for cigar filler blending.

Days to Maturity: 50-56
Spacing: 24-36 inches
Plant Height: 42-50 inches
Leaf Length: 25 inches
Leaf Width: 10-11½ inches
Leaf Count: 16-19

Comments:

ARS-GRIN
PI 552374
TC 489
Yield: 2½ ounces of cured leaf per plant
Nicotine:

Photos: ARS-GRIN, ARS-GRIN

Maryland — Catterton — Maryland

Catterton is classed as a Maryland type. It produces a good yield of mildly flavored leaf that is used mostly for cigarette and pipe blending. Its use in cigars is limited by its tendency to absorb moisture easily. Catterton cooks into a Cavendish useful for taming stronger pipe blends. Its ready absorption of flavoring is useful for making aromatic pipe blends. Catterton is usually stalk-cut and air-cured.

"Resistant to black root rot and partial resistance to Fusarium wilt. High sucker growth. Harvest period for best-cure is very short; matures 7-10 days before typical medium broadleaf varieties."

*ARS-GRIN

Days to Maturity: 54-67
Spacing: 24-36 inches
Plant Height: 34-52 inches
Leaf Length: 24-28 inches
Leaf Width: 13-16 inches
Leaf Count: 17-22

Comments:

ARS-GRIN
PI 551332
TC 494
Yield: 3½ ounces of cured leaf per plant
Nicotine:

Photos: ARS-GRIN, ARS-GRIN, ARS-GRIN

Maryland   Keller   Maryland

Keller is classed as a Maryland type. It produces a good yield of mildly flavored leaf that is used mostly for cigarette and pipe blending. Its use in cigars is limited by its tendency to absorb moisture easily. Keller cooks into a Cavendish useful for taming stronger pipe blends. Its ready absorption of flavoring is useful for making aromatic pipe blends. Keller is usually stalk-cut and air-cured.

Days to Maturity: 48-55
Spacing: 24-36 inches
Plant Height: 35-40½ inches
Leaf Length: 18-24 inches
Leaf Width: 10-11½ inches
Leaf Count: 15-23

Comments:

ARS-GRIN
PI 552669
TC 497
Yield: 2 ounces of cured leaf per plant
Nicotine:

Photos: ARS-GRIN, ARS-GRIN, ARS-GRIN

Maryland   MD A30   Maryland

MD A30 is Maryland type tobacco with yields similar to MD 609. It produces a good yield of mildly flavored leaf that is used mostly for cigarette and pipe blending. Its use in cigars is limited by its tendency to absorb moisture easily. MD A30 cooks into a Cavendish useful for taming stronger pipe blends. Its ready absorption of flavoring is useful for making aromatic pipe blends. Resistant to TMV and Race 0 black shank (Phytophthora parasitica). Grows closely spaced leaves. Similar to cultivars MD 609, MD 872, and MD 201.

[note bumblebee]

Days to Maturity: 63-70
Spacing: 24-36 inches
Plant Height: 60-72 inches
Leaf Length: ~30 inches
Leaf Width: ~14-16 inches
Leaf Count: 23-24
Pedigree
Date released: 1999. A16/A25//L8/3/MD 201

Intellectual Property Rights
Crop Science Registration. GP-53, TOBACCO. Issued: 01 Jul 2000.

Comments:

ARS-GRIN
PI 610239
TC 651
Yield:
Nicotine: ~2.60%

Photos: ARS-GRIN, ARS-GRIN

Maryland   MD 201   Maryland

Maryland 201 is a light air-cured Maryland variety. High resistance to TMV and middle-resistance to Fusarium wilt. The leaves ripen as it reaches maturity and turn a light yellow, making it very easy to cure. It produces a good yield of mildly flavored leaf that is used mostly for cigarette and pipe blending. Its use in cigars is limited by its tendency to absorb moisture easily. MD 201 cooks into a Cavendish useful for taming stronger pipe blends. Its ready absorption of flavoring is useful for making aromatic pipe blends.

Days to Maturity: 55-60
Spacing: 24-36 inches
Plant Height: 60-72 inches
Leaf Length: 26-30 inches
Leaf Width: 9½-12 inches
Leaf Count: 14-16

Pedigree released: 1973. Catterton type breeding line/Maryland 64 breeding line
Intellectual Property Rights:
Crop Science Registration. CV-80, TOBACCO. Issued: 01 Mar 1975.

Comments:

ARS-GRIN
PI 551335
TC 503
Yield:
Nicotine:

Photos: ARS-GRIN, ARS-GRIN, ARS-GRIN

Maryland MD 609 Maryland

Maryland 609 is a medium flavored Maryland class tobacco that is usually stalk-cut and air-cured. It air-cures to a light reddish brown color. It produces a good yield of mildly flavored leaf that is used mostly for cigarette and pipe blending. Its use in cigars is limited by its tendency to absorb moisture easily. MD 609 cooks into a Cavendish useful for taming stronger pipe blends. Its ready absorption of flavoring is useful for making aromatic pipe blends.

Days to Maturity: 53-56
Spacing: 24-36 inches
Plant Height: 34½-44 inches
Leaf Length: 25½-31½ inches
Leaf Width: 11½-13 inches
Leaf Count: 16-22

Pedigree: Maryland Robinson/Florida 301

Intellectual Property Rights
Crop Science Registration. CV-27, TOBACCO. Issued: 01 Jan 1966.

Comments:

ARS-GRIN
PI 552452
TC 505
Yield: 3½ ounces of cured leaf per plant
Nicotine:

Photos: ARS-GRIN, RCAG, RCAG

Maryland — Pennbel 69 — Maryland

Pennbel 69 is a 50+ year old variety, classed by ARS-GRIN as cigar filler, though it appears to be a Maryland-like *"Pennsylvania Seedleaf and Broadleaf Tobacco Type 41,"* air-cured tobacco, developed by the Pennsylvania Dept. of Agriculture. It is usually stalk harvested and air-cures to a medium reddish brown color. It produces a good yield of mildly flavored leaf that is used mostly for cigarette and pipe blending. Its use in cigars is limited by its tendency to absorb moisture easily. Pennbel 69 cooks into a Cavendish useful for taming stronger pipe blends. Its ready absorption of flavoring is useful for making aromatic pipe blends.

Days to Maturity: 65-70
Spacing: 24-36 inches
Plant Height: 39 inches
Leaf Length: 21-26 inches
Leaf Width: 11½-13½ inches
Leaf Count: 15-21

Comments:

ARS-GRIN
PI 552404
TC 121
Yield: 2 ounces of cured leaf per plant
Nicotine:

Photos: Northwood Seeds, ARS-GRIN, Northwood Seeds

Maryland — Thompson — Maryland

Thompson is a Maryland class, air-cured tobacco. The leaves air-cure to a medium reddish brown. It produces a good yield of mildly flavored leaf that is used mostly for cigarette and pipe blending. Its use in cigars is limited by its tendency to absorb moisture easily. Thompson cooks into a Cavendish useful for taming stronger pipe blends. Its ready absorption of flavoring is useful for making aromatic pipe blends.

Days to Maturity: 58-78
Spacing: 24-36 inches
Plant Height: 30 inches
Leaf Length: 23-24½ inches
Leaf Width: 8-12 inches
Leaf Count: 15-18

Comments:

ARS-GRIN
PI 552763
TC 515
Yield: 2 ounces of cured leaf per plant
Nicotine:

Photos: Northwood Seeds, ARS-GRIN, ARS-GRIN

Oriental   **Adiyaman**   **Oriental**

Adiyaman is an Oriental variety that originated in the south-central region of Turkey. Its long and narrow leaves are described as "ox-tongue", or sirdili. The texture of Adiyaman strain is moderately thick. Adiyaman is generally used in blends to bring them fullness, sweetness and aroma. Usually sun-cured. Useful for cigarette and pipe blending. Closer spacing and minimal fertilizer use will produce smaller, more fragrant and more traditional Turkish leaf. Wider spacing and increased fertilization will produce much larger leaf that lacks its Oriental character. Adiyaman is the district in which the city of Çelikhan is located, and the two tobaccos are quite similar (and sometimes conflated).

Days to Maturity: 32-42
Spacing: 6-12 inches
Plant Height: 20½-21 inches
Leaf Length: 14½-19 inches
Leaf Width: 6-7½ inches
Leaf Count: 12-14

Comments:

ARS-GRIN
PI 494145
TI 1663
Yield: ounces of cured leaf per plant
Nicotine: 1.7-2.0%

Photos: ARS-GRIN, ARS-GRIN

Oriental — Alma Ata 315 — Oriental

Alma Ata 315 was developed in Alma-Ata USSR, (now Almaty, Kazakhstan) at the Alma-Ata Tobacco State Farm about 1950. Alma Ata 315 produces a mild and very aromatic smoke. Usually sun-cured. Useful for cigarette and pipe blending. Closer spacing and minimal fertilizer use will produce smaller, more fragrant and more traditional Turkish leaf. Wider spacing and increased fertilization will produce much larger leaf that lacks its Oriental character.

Days to Maturity: 40-90
Spacing: 6-12 inches
Plant Height: 36-54 inches
Leaf Length: 16 inches
Leaf Width: 8-16 inches
Leaf Count: 12-16

Pedigree: complex crosses involving *N. glutinosa*, Dubek 44, Samsun 57 and powdery mildew-resistant Trapezonds 214 and coastal 117.

Comments:

Yield: 1½ ounces of cured leaf per plant
Nicotine:

Photos: Northwood Seeds, Northwood Seeds

Oriental — American 3 — Oriental

American 3 is a large, heavy-producing Oriental tobacco, developed in Crimea. American 3 is is said to be "drought tolerant, scorch tolerant." Air-cures to a light yellow brown. Usually sun-cured. Useful for cigarette and pipe blending. Closer spacing and minimal fertilizer use will produce smaller, more fragrant and more traditional Turkish leaf. Wider spacing and increased fertilization will produce much larger leaf that lacks its Oriental character. Those considerations may or may not be of concern with this variety.

Days to Maturity: 57-70
Spacing: 6-12 inches
Plant Height: 47 inches
Leaf Length: 16-20 inches
Leaf Width: 9-14 inches
Leaf Count: 22-32

Pedigree: (572 x American x *Nicotiana sylvestris* x Trapezond 10)

Comments:

Yield:
Nicotine: 2.7-3.0%

Photos: Northwood Seeds, Northwood Seeds

Oriental — American 14 — Oriental

American 14 is a genetically stable, Oriental/Bright Leaf cross, imported from Ukraine. American 14 is said to be "drought tolerant and scorch tolerant." Air cures to a light yellow brown. Usually sun-cured. Useful for cigarette and pipe blending. Closer spacing and minimal fertilizer use will produce smaller, more fragrant and more traditional Turkish leaf. Wider spacing and increased fertilization will produce much larger leaf that lacks its Oriental character. Those considerations may or may not be of concern with this variety.

Days to Maturity: 60-70
Spacing: 6-12 inches
Plant Height: 71 inches
Leaf Length: 12 inches
Leaf Width: 3 inches
Leaf Count: 30-33

Pedigree: (Dubek new × American 3)

Comments:

Yield:
Nicotine:

Photos: Northwood Seeds, Northwood Seeds

Oriental — American 26 — Oriental

American 26 is an early maturing, sun-cured or air-cured, aromatic Oriental variety of tobacco, developed in Crimea. It is said to be "drought-resistant and resistant to burning." American 26 sun-cures to a bright golden yellow or air-cures to a light golden brown. Useful for cigarette and pipe blending. Closer spacing and minimal fertilizer use will produce smaller, more fragrant and more traditional Oriental leaf. Wider spacing and increased fertilization will produce much larger leaf that lacks its Oriental character. Those considerations may or may not be of concern with this variety.

Days to Maturity: 56-73
Spacing: 6-12 inches
Plant Height: 47 inches
Leaf Length: 10 inches
Leaf Width: 6 inches
Leaf Count: 20

Pedigree: (American 3 × (New Dubec × Dubec 44) × Trapezond 19)

Comments:

Yield:
Nicotine:

Photos: Northwood Seeds, Northwood Seeds

American 63

Oriental   **Oriental**

American 63 is a high yielding, aromatic Oriental air-cured or sun-cured variety from Crimea. It can be blended or used alone for cigarette or pipe blends. It is said to be "drought tolerant and scorch tolerant." Closer spacing and minimal fertilizer use will produce smaller, more fragrant and more traditional Turkish leaf. Wider spacing and increased fertilization will produce much larger leaf that lacks its Oriental character. Those considerations may or may not be of concern with this variety.

Days to Maturity: 65-84
Spacing: 6-12 inches
Plant Height: 43 inches
Leaf Length: 12½ inches
Leaf Width: 7 inches
Leaf Count: 18-22

Comments:

Yield:
Nicotine:

Photos: Northwood Seeds, Northwood Seeds

Oriental — American 572 — Oriental

American 572 is an Oriental variety that can be sun-cured or air-cured. Considered one of the best varieties of "American" developed in Ukraine. Useful for cigarette and pipe blending. Closer spacing and minimal fertilizer use will produce smaller, more fragrant and more traditional Oriental leaf. Wider spacing and increased fertilization will produce much larger leaf that lacks its Oriental character. Those considerations may or may not be of concern with this variety.

Days to Maturity: ?
Spacing: 6-12 inches
Plant Height: 36-40 inches
Leaf Length: 18 inches
Leaf Width: 10 inches
Leaf Count: 14-16

Comments:

Yield:
Nicotine:

Photos: Northwood Seeds, Northwood Seeds

Oriental   Anatolian   Oriental

Anatolian is "perhaps" Muş, an Oriental tobacco from the area of the city of Muş, in eastern central Turkey. (The seed was originally collected in Turkey, then imported into Ukraine.) The color of the cured leaf ranges from lemon yellow to orange brown. It's main use is in cigarette blends. It can be sun-cured or air-cured. Useful for cigarette and pipe blending. Closer spacing and minimal fertilizer use will produce smaller, more fragrant and more traditional Turkish leaf. Wider spacing and increased fertilization will produce much larger leaf that lacks its Oriental character.

Days to Maturity: 45-50
Spacing: 6-12 inches
Plant Height: 30 inches
Leaf Length: 15-20 inches
Leaf Width: 6-9 inches
Leaf Count: 12-15

Comments:

ARS-GRIN
PI 537052 (Muş)
TI 1726 (Muş)
Yield:
Nicotine:

Photos: ARS-GRIN, ARS-GRIN, ARS-GRIN

Oriental　　Bafra　　Oriental

Bafra is an Oriental tobacco from the northern coast of Turkey, grown in the districts of Bafra and Alaçam, near the city of Samsun. ARS-GRIN incorrectly classes Bafra as a Primitive. Like Samsun, Bafra is a heart-shaped, petiolate leaf. It tends to be milder than Samsun, but spicier than most Basma types. Usually sun-cured. Useful for cigarette and pipe blending, it can be smoked alone in cigarettes. Closer spacing and minimal fertilizer use will produce smaller, more fragrant and more traditional Turkish leaf. Wider spacing and increased fertilization will produce much larger leaf that lacks its Oriental character.

Days to Maturity: 50-58
Spacing: 6-12 inches
Plant Height: 48-52 inches
Leaf Length: 10-13 inches
Leaf Width: 5-8 inches
Leaf Count: 24-32

Comments:

ARS-GRIN
PI 494146
TI 1664
Yield: ounces of cured leaf per plant
Nicotine: 0.8-1.2%

Photos: ARS-GRIN, ARS-GRIN, ARS-GRIN

Oriental — Bahia — Oriental

Bahia is the **cigar** variety that is the famous Mata Fina leaf of Brazil. ARS-GRIN has incorrectly classified this as an Oriental. Bahia should be planted at spacing typical for cigar leaf—24-36 inches between plants. It is air-cured. Since low-fires are used in the curing barns of Brazil, the commercial leaf takes on a slightly smoky aroma. Bahia makes wonderful cigar wrapper, binder and filler.

Days to Maturity: 35-42
Spacing: **24-36** inches
Plant Height: 29-48 inches
Leaf Length: 14-17½ inches
Leaf Width: 8½-11 inches
Leaf Count: 15-18

Home-grown Bahia ligero puro

Comments:

ARS-GRIN
PI 260362
TI 1416
Yield: 1-2 ounces of cured leaf per plant
Nicotine: 0.2% (nornicotine: 1.54%) [perhaps reversed by ARS-GRIN]

Photos: RCAG, ARS-GRIN, RCAG, RCAG

Oriental — Baiano — Oriental

Baiano is a Hungarian class tobacco used in cigars and pipe tobaccos. It is a heavy producer, with large, thick leaves. Little to no suckering. Leaves are a dark green, closely spaced on the stalk, and grow upright. Baiano has a densely packed flower head, that does not extend above the plant. This trait generally defines the "Hungarian" class. Mature plants tolerate frost well. Curiously, Baiano is a Brazilian tobacco growing region, and the only Baiano accession at ARS-GRIN was acquired from Brazil. This variety may have nothing to do with Hungary (or the former Austro-Hungarian Empire), and is certainly not an Oriental tobacco.

Days to Maturity: 47-65
Spacing: 24-36 inches
Plant Height: 37½-57½ inches
Leaf Length: 10-19 inches
Leaf Width: 10-11½ inches
Leaf Count: 12-19

Comments:

ARS-GRIN
PI 404979
TI 128
Yield: 2-4 ounces of cured leaf per plant
Nicotine: 1.37%

Photos: ARS-GRIN, ARS-GRIN, ARS-GRIN

Oriental — Balikesir — Oriental

Balikesir is a Basma-type Oriental variety from the western coastal plains of Turkey. It sun-cures to a light tan color or air-cures to a dark coco brown. Usually sun-cured. Useful for cigarette and pipe blending. Closer spacing and minimal fertilizer use will produce smaller, more fragrant and more traditional Turkish leaf. Wider spacing and increased fertilization will produce much larger leaf that lacks its Oriental character.

Days to Maturity: 53-73
Spacing: 6-12 inches
Plant Height: 31-37 inches
Leaf Length: 13-15 inches
Leaf Width: 7½-9 inches
Leaf Count: 22

Comments:

ARS-GRIN
PI 494147
TI 1665
Yield:
Nicotine:

Photos: ARS-GRIN, RCAG, RCAG

Oriental — Basma — Oriental

Basma is both an Oriental tobacco variety as well as a type or family or Oriental tobacco. [The word likely derives from the Ottoman practice of *pressing* the small leaves into a tidy, rectangular bale, called pressed tobacco.] The leaves are small, ovoid, with a pointed tip. Basma tobacco originated in Greece. It is known for its sweet and aromatic taste, when sun-cured. Usually sun-cured. Useful for cigarette and pipe blending. Closer spacing and minimal fertilizer use will produce smaller, more fragrant and more traditional Turkish leaf. Wider spacing and increased fertilization will produce much larger leaf that lacks its Oriental character. With all Basma types, aim for a plant height of about 3 feet, for the best quality.

Days to Maturity: 60
Spacing: 6-12 inches
Plant Height: 36-58½ inches
Leaf Length: 9-13 inches
Leaf Width: 3-7½ inches
Leaf Count: 20-24

Comments:

ARS-GRIN
PI 494148
TI 1666
Yield: ounces of cured leaf per plant
Nicotine: ~1%

Photos: Basma, ARS-GRIN, ARS-GRIN

Oriental — Bursa — Oriental

Bursa is heavy-producing Oriental variety, grown southeast of Istanbul. Dark green, spade-shaped leaves. The unique flavor is spicy and sweet and the smoke is fragrant and aromatic. Usually sun-cured, but may also be air-cured. Useful for cigarette and pipe blending.

Days to Maturity: 63-70
Spacing: 24-36 inches
Plant Height: 66 inches
Leaf Length: 16 inches
Leaf Width: 10-11 inches
Leaf Count: 30-34

Comments:

ARS-GRIN
PI 481863
TI 1650
Yield:
Nicotine:

Photos: ARS-GRIN, ARS-GRIN, ARS-GRIN

Oriental — Canik — Oriental

Canik is an Oriental variety of tobacco grown in the vicinity of Samsun, Turkey, but is quite different from the Samsun variety. (Canik grows sessile, ox-tongue leaves, whereas Samsun produces petiolate, heart-shaped leaves.) Canik has a mild, sweet and spicy taste. Usually sun-cured. Useful for cigarette and pipe blending. Closer spacing and minimal fertilizer use will produce smaller, more fragrant and more traditional Turkish leaf. Wider spacing and increased fertilization will produce much larger leaf that lacks its Oriental character.

Days to Maturity: 49-55
Spacing: 6-12 inches
Plant Height: 45 inches
Leaf Length: 13-16 inches
Leaf Width: 6-7 inches
Leaf Count: 25-30

Comments:

ARS-GRIN
PI 481857
TI 1644
Yield: 2 ounces of cured leaf per plant
Nicotine: ~1.3%

Photos: ARS-GRIN, Northwood Seeds, ARS-GRIN

Oriental — Çelikhan — Oriental

Çelikhan is a refined variety of Adiyaman Oriental tobacco originating in south-central area of Turkey. (Çelikhan itself is a rural area within Adiyaman Province.) Usually sun-cured. Useful for cigarette and pipe blending. Closer spacing and minimal fertilizer use will produce smaller, more fragrant and more traditional Turkish leaf. Wider spacing and increased fertilization will produce much larger leaf that lacks its Oriental character.

Days to Maturity: 40-52
Spacing: 6-12 inches
Plant Height: 12-27 inches
Leaf Length: 12-18 inches
Leaf Width: 3-5 inches
Leaf Count: 11-16

Comments:

ARS-GRIN
PI 494151
TI 1669
Yield:
Nicotine: 1.7-2.0%

Photos: RCAG, ARS-GRIN, RCAG

Oriental   Citir   Oriental

Citir is an Oriental variety similar to Izmir. Usually sun-cured. Useful for cigarette and pipe blending. Closer spacing and minimal fertilizer use will produce smaller, more fragrant and more traditional Turkish leaf. Wider spacing and increased fertilization will produce much larger leaf that lacks its Oriental character.

Days to Maturity: 60-63
Spacing: 6-12 inches
Plant Height: 52 inches
Leaf Length: 8-14 inches
Leaf Width: 5-6½ inches
Leaf Count: 33-40

Comments:

ARS-GRIN
PI 481864
TI 1651
Yield:
Nicotine: ~1%

Photos: ARS-GRIN, ARS-GRIN, ARS-GRIN

Oriental — Djebel 174 — Oriental

Djebel 174 is an Oriental Basma-type variety from Bulgaria. It is also grown in the mountains of Morocco. Djebel tobacco traditionally refers to those Oriental tobaccos coming from steeper mountain areas. [as opposed to yaka, from the lower slopes] Usually sun-cured. Useful for cigarette and pipe blending. Closer spacing and minimal fertilizer use will produce smaller, more fragrant and more traditional Turkish leaf. Wider spacing and increased fertilization will produce much larger leaf that lacks its Oriental character.

Days to Maturity: 44-97
Spacing: 6-12 inches
Plant Height: 37-55 inches
Leaf Length: 13-21½ inches
Leaf Width: 7½-13 inches
Leaf Count: 15-18

Comments:

ARS-GRIN
PI 321709
TI 1492
Yield: 2½-3 ounces of cured leaf per plant
Nicotine: 4.28%

Photos: RCAG, ARS-GRIN, RCAG

Oriental — Dukat Crimean — Oriental

Dukat Crimean (Crimean Ducat, or Crimean gold coin) appears to be a Basma-type Oriental variety. The air-cured leaf is a reddish-brown color. Imported from Ukraine. Usual curing method is unknown. Useful for cigarette and pipe blending. Closer spacing and minimal fertilizer use will produce smaller, more fragrant and more traditional Oriental leaf. Wider spacing and increased fertilization will produce much larger leaf that lacks its Oriental character. Those considerations may or may not be of concern with this variety.

Days to Maturity: ?
Spacing: 6-12 inches
Plant Height: 60-72 inches
Leaf Length: 16½ inches
Leaf Width: 7 inches
Leaf Count: 23-25

Comments:

Yield:
Nicotine:

Photos: Northwood Seeds, Northwood Seeds

Oriental   Düzce   Oriental

Düzce is an Oriental variety once grown in the Düzce province of Turkey. Düzce province rests on the Black Sea coast, about 120 miles east of Istanbul. Düzce tobacco is no longer grown there. It appears to be an intermediate type between Basma (sessile leaf base) and a Samsun-type Oriental (with a fringed petiole). Usually sun-cured. Useful for cigarette and pipe blending. Closer spacing and minimal fertilizer use will produce smaller, more fragrant and more traditional Turkish leaf. Wider spacing and increased fertilization will produce much larger leaf that lacks its Oriental character. (The author planted 26 Düzce plants, evenly spaced in a 5' x 6' bed shown in photos.)

Days to Maturity: 53-60
Spacing: 6-12 inches
Plant Height: 60 inches
Leaf Length: 11½-14 inches
Leaf Width: 7-9 inches
Leaf Count: 15-28

Comments:

ARS-GRIN
PI 494152
TI 1670
Yield:
Nicotine:

Home-grown, sun-cured, kilned Düzce

Photos: all RCAG

Oriental   Ege   Oriental

Ege is an Oriental variety that appears to be a type of Izmir, grown in the Aegean region of Turkey. It is fine-ribbed and has a sweet, aromatic taste. Usually sun-cured. Useful for cigarette and pipe blending. Closer spacing and minimal fertilizer use will produce smaller, more fragrant and more traditional Turkish leaf. Wider spacing and increased fertilization will produce much larger leaf that lacks its Oriental character.

Days to Maturity: 55-60
Spacing: 6-12 inches
Plant Height: 33-42 inches
Leaf Length: 11-16 inches
Leaf Width: 6-9 inches
Leaf Count: 16-20

Comments:

ARS-GRIN
PI 481855
TI 1642
Yield:
Nicotine: 1.0%

Photos: ARS-GRIN, Northwood Seeds, ARS-GRIN

Oriental — Harmanli — Oriental

Harmanli is said to be an Oriental variety grown in Bulgaria. (The town of Harmanli is within 30 miles of the border with both Turkey and Greece.) Likely a semi-Oriental. This is a very large-growing tobacco for a supposed Oriental type. Harmanli is an aromatic tobacco with a unique flavor and high yields. Resistant to tobacco mosaic virus. Can be sun-cured or air-cured. Useful for cigarette and pipe blending.

Days to Maturity: 70
Spacing: 24-36 inches
Plant Height: 71-108 inches
Leaf Length: 11-24 inches
Leaf Width: 5-16 inches
Leaf Count: 28-35

Comments:

Yield:
Nicotine: 1.5-1.75%

Photos: Northwood Seeds, Northwood Seeds

Oriental — Harmanliiska Basma 163 — Oriental

Harmanliiska Basma 163 is a Bulgarian Oriental tobacco. It produces a fragrant smoke. Can be sun-cured or air-cured. Useful for cigarette and pipe blending. Closer spacing and minimal fertilizer use will produce smaller, more fragrant and more traditional Oriental leaf. Wider spacing and increased fertilization will produce much larger leaf that lacks its Oriental character.

Days to Maturity: 45-60
Spacing: 6-12 inches
Plant Height: 43-53 inches
Leaf Length: 14½-18 inches
Leaf Width: 8½-14 inches
Leaf Count: 16-26

Comments:

ARS-GRIN
PI 286819
TI 1378
Yield: 1-2 ounces of cured leaf per plant
Nicotine: 2.18%

Photos: Northwood Seeds, ARS-GRIN, ARS-GRIN

Oriental Herzegovina Flor Oriental

Herzegovina Flor is a large leaf variety of Oriental tobacco. It is a sweet tobacco with a pleasant aroma. Can be sun-cured or air-cured. Useful for cigarette and pipe blending. Closer spacing and minimal fertilizer use will produce smaller, more fragrant and more traditional Oriental leaf. Wider spacing and increased fertilization will produce much larger leaf that lacks its Oriental character. Those considerations may or may not be of concern with this variety.

Days to Maturity: 45-50
Spacing: 6-12 inches
Plant Height: 48-90 inches
Leaf Length: 20-22 inches
Leaf Width: 12-14 inches
Leaf Count: 15-16

Comments:

Yield: 2-3 ounces of cured leaf per plant
Nicotine:

Photos: Northwood Seeds, Northwood Seeds

Oriental — Incekara — Oriental

Incekara is one of the many variants of Izmir variety. [Izmir was once the ancient city of Smyrna.] It is a Basma-type Oriental tobacco grown in the coastal area of western Turkey. Resistant to blue mold. Usually sun-cured. Useful for cigarette and pipe blending. Closer spacing and minimal fertilizer use will produce smaller, more fragrant and more traditional Turkish leaf. Wider spacing and increased fertilization will produce much larger leaf that lacks its Oriental character.

Days to Maturity: 55
Spacing: 6-12 inches
Plant Height: 27-48 inches
Leaf Length: 10-14 inches
Leaf Width: 5-7 inches
Leaf Count: 20-22

Comments:

ARS-GRIN
PI 481868
TI 1656
Yield:
Nicotine:

Photos: ARS-GRIN, ARS-GRIN, ARS-GRIN

Oriental — Izmir-Karabaglar — Oriental

Izmir-Karabaglar is one of the many variants of Izmir variety. [Izmir was once the ancient city of Smyrna.] Karabaglar is in the southern part of Izmir province. It is a Basma-type Oriental tobacco. Usually sun-cured. Useful for cigarette and pipe blending. Closer spacing and minimal fertilizer use will produce smaller, more fragrant and more traditional Turkish leaf. Wider spacing and increased fertilization will produce much larger leaf that lacks its Oriental character.

Not to be confused with Karabaglar Rustica.

Days to Maturity: 55
Spacing: 6-12 inches
Plant Height: 51-52 inches
Leaf Length: 8½-14½ inches
Leaf Width: 4-7½ inches
Leaf Count: 22-37

Comments:

ARS-GRIN
PI 494158
TI 1676
Yield:
Nicotine:

Photos: RCAG, ARS-GRIN, RCAG

Oriental — Izmir Ozbas — Oriental

Izmir Ozbas is one of the many variants of Izmir variety. [Izmir was once the ancient city of Smyrna.] This variety uniquely displays an upturned rim curvature along the edges of each leaf. It is a Basma-type Oriental tobacco. Usually sun-cured. Useful for cigarette and pipe blending. Closer spacing and minimal fertilizer use will produce smaller, more fragrant and more traditional Turkish leaf. Wider spacing and increased fertilization will produce much larger leaf that lacks its Oriental character.

Upturned leaf rim

Days to Maturity: 47-67
Spacing: 6-12 inches
Plant Height: 58-68 inches
Leaf Length: 13-14½ inches
Leaf Width: 8-9 inches
Leaf Count: 25-31

Comments:

ARS-GRIN
PI 494157
TI 1675
Yield:
Nicotine:

Photos: ARS-GRIN, ARS-GRIN, RCAG, RCAG

Oriental — Izmir (Lebanon) — Oriental

Izmir (Lebanon) is an unidentified variant of Izmir that was grown from seed collected in Lebanon in early 2011. The leaves are a lighter green than Izmir Ozbas but otherwise similar in size and shape. The flowers are a creamy white. The leaves air-cure to a light tan brown or sun-cure to a light gold yellow. Usually sun-cured. Useful for cigarette and pipe blending. Closer spacing and minimal fertilizer use will produce smaller, more fragrant and more traditional Turkish leaf. Wider spacing and increased fertilization will produce much larger leaf that lacks its Oriental character.

Days to Maturity: 50
Spacing: 6-12 inches
Plant Height: 72 inches
Leaf Length: ~14 inches
Leaf Width: ~9 inches
Leaf Count: ~14-20

Comments:

Yield:
Nicotine:

Photos: Northwood Seeds, Northwood Seeds, Northwood Seeds

Oriental — Japan 8 — Oriental

Japan 8 is a very sweet, dark Oriental tobacco, said to have low nicotine content. It grows as a compact shrub, with long, narrow leaves. It can be air-cured or sun-cured, though usually sun-cured. It is useful for cigarette or pipe blending. Air-cured leaves are a deep brown, and produce a mild smoke with a licorice-like flavor. The flowers are a creamy white.

[The author suspects that this might be closer to an Orinoco-type flue-cured variety, rather than an Oriental.]

Days to Maturity: 65-81
Spacing: ? inches
Plant Height: 72 inches
Leaf Length: 14-24 inches
Leaf Width: 4-10 inches
Leaf Count: 24-28

Comments:

Yield:
Nicotine:

Photos: Northwood Seeds, Northwood Seeds

Oriental Krumovgrad 58 Oriental

Krumovgrad 58 is a Basma-type Oriental variety grown in Bulgaria. The lower leaves begin to ripen about 2 weeks before the plant reaches bloom. The leaves sun-cure to a light orange-yellow, with a fine flavor, pleasant taste, and good burning quality. Krumovgrad 58 accounts for 10% of the oriental tobacco grown in Bulgaria. Resistant to "TSWV". Usually sun-cured. Useful for cigarette and pipe blending. Closer spacing and minimal fertilizer use will produce smaller, more fragrant and more traditional Oriental leaf. Wider spacing and increased fertilization will produce much larger leaf that lacks its Oriental character.

Days to Maturity: 65-70
Spacing: 6-12 inches
Plant Height: 54-72 inches
Leaf Length: 9½-14 inches
Leaf Width: 5-8 inches
Leaf Count: 24-37

Comments:

Yield:
Nicotine:

Photos: Northwood Seeds, Northwood Seeds

Oriental — Kumanovo — Oriental

Kumanovo is a full flavored Hungarian variety used in cigar and pipe tobaccos. It forms a very dense cauliflower-type flower head which is quite showy in its appearance. A good choice for growers who want an attractive garden plant and want to produce tobacco. Usually air-cured.

Days to Maturity: 50
Spacing: 18 inches
Plant Height: 33-42 inches
Leaf Length: 16 inches
Leaf Width: 12 inches
Leaf Count: 16-19

Comments:

Yield:
Nicotine:

Photos: Stewart Cranston, Stewart Cranston

Oriental — Lattaquie 92 — Oriental

Lattaquie 92 is a very early maturing Oriental tobacco from France. Once blooming has started, the plants keep producing more flowers for 2-3 months. It is a good plant for small planting areas. Lattaquie 92 is a dual purpose plant to grow for the flower garden. Can be sun-cured or air-cured. Useful for cigarette and pipe blending. Closer spacing and minimal fertilizer use will produce smaller, more fragrant and more traditional Turkish leaf. Wider spacing and increased fertilization will produce much larger leaf that lacks its Oriental character.

Days to Maturity: 30-69
Spacing: 6-12 inches
Plant Height: 24-47 inches
Leaf Length: 8-24½ inches
Leaf Width: 4-12 inches
Leaf Count: 21

Comments:

ARS-GRIN
PI 483069
TI 1658
Yield:
Nicotine:

Photos: Northwood Seeds, Northwood Seeds

Oriental   Meechurinski   Oriental

Meechurinski is a Russian Oriental tobacco developed by Ivan Michurin, by crossing early Bulgarian tobacco and small leaf Sumatra. It is an early maturing variety, and a small plant. Leaves air-cure to a light brown, making a fragrant smoke. Grows well in sandy soils. Useful for cigarette and pipe blending. Closer spacing and minimal fertilizer use will produce smaller, more fragrant and more traditional Turkish leaf. Wider spacing and increased fertilization will produce much larger leaf that lacks its Oriental character.

Days to Maturity: 35-40
Spacing: 12 inches
Plant Height: 24 inches
Leaf Length: 10 inches
Leaf Width: 6 inches
Leaf Count: 6-8

Comments:

Yield:
Nicotine:

Photos: Northwood Seeds, Northwood Seeds

Oriental   Mutki   Oriental

Mutki is a Turkish Oriental that originated in eastern central Turkey. It is noticeably less sweet than Basma types. Usually sun-cured. Mostly used for cigarette and pipe blending. Even when sun-cured, it can serve as an interesting wrapper for small cigars. Mutki tip leaf (ootz) is intensely flavorful. Closer spacing and minimal fertilizer use will produce smaller, more fragrant and more traditional Turkish leaf. Wider spacing and increased fertilization will produce much larger leaf that lacks its Oriental character.

Days to Maturity: 53-71
Spacing: 12-16 inches
Plant Height: 46 inches
Leaf Length: 19-22 inches
Leaf Width: 10-13 inches
Leaf Count: 16-18

Home-grown, sun-cured Mutki wrapper

Comments:

ARS-GRIN
PI 494159
TI TI 1677
Yield:
Nicotine:

Photos: all RCAG

Oriental — Native 9 (Bolivia) — Oriental

Native 9 is an unnamed "Oriental" variety originating in Bolivia, donated to ARS-GRIN in 1956. Likely typical of native tobacco varieties (like Flojo) common to the Andes high-plains. Usually air-cured, but can be fire-cured. Uses are for strong cigarette filler, cigar filler and oral preparations. The ARS-GRIN class of "Oriental" seems doubtful.

Days to Maturity: 47-60
Spacing: 24-36 inches
Plant Height: 40-60 inches
Leaf Length: 14½-20 inches
Leaf Width: 8-10 inches
Leaf Count: 14-18

Comments:

ARS-GRIN
PI 235561
TI 1302
Yield: 1-3 ounces of cured leaf per plant
Nicotine: 2.2%

Photos: ARS-GRIN, ARS-GRIN, Northwood Seeds

Oriental   Nevrokop 5   Oriental

Nevrokop 5 is a Macedonian type Oriental variety grown in Bulgaria. Cured leaves have a light color with a sweet and tasty smoke. Usually sun-cured. Useful for cigarette and pipe blending. Closer spacing and minimal fertilizer use will produce smaller, more fragrant and more traditional Oriental leaf. Wider spacing and increased fertilization will produce much larger leaf that lacks its Oriental character.

Days to Maturity: 61-97
Spacing: 12 inches
Plant Height: 53-60 inches
Leaf Length: 12-18 inches
Leaf Width: 6-10 inches
Leaf Count: 17-25

Comments:

ARS-GRIN
PI 286823
TI 1382
Yield: 1¼-3 ounces of cured leaf per plant
Nicotine: 2.87%

Photos: ARS-GRIN, ARS-GRIN, ARS-GRIN

Oriental — Prancak N-1 — Oriental

Prancak N-1 is an Oriental tobacco developed on the Indonesian island of Madura. Prancak N-1 combines characteristics of both its parents. The result is a light, Izmir-like leaf that readily sun-cures to a golden color, and can also be flue-cured to produce sweet, bright leaf. It is usually sun-cured. Useful for cigarette and pipe blending. Closer spacing and minimal fertilizer use will produce smaller, more fragrant and more traditional Oriental leaf. Wider spacing and increased fertilization will produce much larger leaf that lacks its Oriental character.

Pedigree:
Date released: 2004. Backcross pollination of Prancak 95 and Ismir Orient

Days to Maturity: 55-80
Spacing: 12 inches
Plant Height: 18½-36 inches
Leaf Length: 10½-15 inches
Leaf Width: 5½-9 inches
Leaf Count: 11-20

Home-grown sun-cured Prancak N-1

Home-grown flue-cured Prancak N-1

Comments:

ARS-GRIN
PI *none*
TC 666
Yield:
Nicotine: 1.76%

Photos: all RCAG

Oriental — Prilep 66-9/7 — Oriental

Prilep 66-9/7 is an Oriental variety developed and grown in North Macedonia. The leaves are upturned and densely packed on the stalk. Its light green leaves are crinkled in appearance. Lower leaves begin to ripen about 2 weeks before flowering begins. Leaves sun-cure to a yellow-orange color and air-cure to a light orange-brown. This tobacco is medium in strength, with a full, sweet taste, and intense aroma. Usually sun-cured. Prilep flue-cures beautifully into what has been described as "tobacco candy." Useful for cigarette and pipe blending. Closer spacing and minimal fertilizer use will produce smaller, more fragrant and more traditional Oriental leaf. Wider spacing and increased fertilization will produce much larger leaf that lacks some of its Oriental character.

Days to Maturity: 70-77
Spacing: 12 inches
Plant Height: 51-52 inches
Leaf Length: 10-15 inches
Leaf Width: 6-8 inches
Leaf Count: 50-55

Home-grown, flue-cured Prilep 66-9/7

Comments:

Yield: 2½-3 ounces of cured leaf per plant
Nicotine: 1.00-2.38%

Photos: all RCAG

Oriental — Prilep 79-94 — Oriental

Prilep 79-94 is an Oriental variety developed and grown in North Macedonia. Similar to Prilep 66-9/7, with slightly thinner leaf. The leaves are upturned and densely packed on the stalk. Its light green leaves are crinkled in appearance. Lower leaves begin to ripen about 2 weeks before flowering begins. Leaves sun-cure to a yellow-orange color and air-cure to a light orange-brown. This tobacco is medium in strength, with a full, sweet taste, and intense aroma. Usually sun-cured. Useful for cigarette and pipe blending. Closer spacing and minimal fertilizer use will produce smaller, more fragrant and more traditional Oriental leaf. Wider spacing and increased fertilization will produce much larger leaf that lacks some of its Oriental character.

Days to Maturity: 70-76
Spacing: 12 inches
Plant Height: 50-53 inches
Leaf Length: 10½ inches
Leaf Width: 6-7 inches
Leaf Count: 50-55

Comments:

Yield: 2 ounces of cured leaf per plant
Nicotine: 1.00-2.38%

Photos: all RCAG

Tobacco Plant Varieties for Home Growers

Oriental   Rejina   Oriental

Rejina (queen) is a Romanian Oriental tobacco. It can be sun-cured or air-cured. Useful for cigarette and pipe blending. Closer spacing and minimal fertilizer use will produce smaller, more fragrant and more traditional Oriental leaf. Wider spacing and increased fertilization will produce much larger leaf that lacks its Oriental character.

Days to Maturity: 36-60
Spacing: 6-12 inches
Plant Height: 48½-51½ inches
Leaf Length: 17-22 inches
Leaf Width: 8-12 inches
Leaf Count: 14-18

Comments:

ARS-GRIN
PI 405521
TI 380
Yield: 1½-2 ounces of cured leaf per plant
Nicotine: 2.62

Photos: Northwood Seeds, ARS-GRIN

| Oriental | Samsun | Oriental |

Samsun originated in the Samsun region of Turkey near the Black Sea. Characteristic, heart-shaped leaf with a fringed petiole (leaf stem). Usually sun-cured. Useful for cigarette and pipe blending. Closer spacing and minimal fertilizer use will produce smaller, more fragrant and more traditional Turkish leaf. Wider spacing and increased fertilization will produce much larger leaf that lacks its Oriental character.

Days to Maturity: 50-70
Spacing: 12-16 inches
Plant Height: 42-72 inches
Leaf Length: 16-19 inches
Leaf Width: 11½-15 inches
Leaf Count: 18-28

Comments:

ARS-GRIN
PI 552747
TC 536
Yield: 1½ ounces of cured leaf per plant
Nicotine:

Photos: ARS-GRIN, ARS-GRIN, ARS-GRIN

Oriental   Samsun Maden   Oriental

Samsun Maden is distinct from Samsun. Samsun Maden is an Oriental variety also from the Black Sea region near the port city of Samsun. It is considered somewhat smoother and milder than Samsun. Usually sun-cured. Useful for cigarette and pipe blending. Closer spacing and minimal fertilizer use will produce smaller, more fragrant and more traditional Turkish leaf. Wider spacing and increased fertilization will produce much larger leaf that lacks its Oriental character.

PI 494161

Days to Maturity: 49-53
Spacing: 12-16 inches
Plant Height: 33-46 inches
Leaf Length: 12-13½ inches
Leaf Width: 7 inches
Leaf Count: 21-24

PI 481860

Comments:

ARS-GRIN [two apparently identical accessions]
(From 2 different universities in Turkey)
a) PI 481860; b) PI 494161
a) TI 1647; b) TI 1679
Yield:
Nicotine:

Photos: sources a) ARS-GRIN, b) ARS-GRIN, a) ARS-GRIN

Oriental — Shirazi — Oriental

Shirazi is an Oriental variety from the area of Shiraz, in southwestern Iran. It is rather different from other Oriental varieties. Shirazi is flavorful and potent. Usually sun-cured. Useful for cigarette and pipe blending. A distinctive feature of the leaves is cupping of the upper leaf, unrelated to calcium deficiency or soil pH.

Days to Maturity: 43-60
Spacing: 24 inches
Plant Height: 45-59 inches
Leaf Length: 8½-22 inches
Leaf Width: 5-10½ inches
Leaf Count: 12-17

Comments:

ARS-GRIN
PI 483078
TI 1659
Yield:
Nicotine:

Photos: RCAG, ARS-GRIN, RCAG

Oriental | Simox | Oriental

Simox is a Hungarian variety from the area of Serbia and Montenegro. It is similar to Kumanovo in its growth habit and plant form. Leaves cure to a dark brown, and make a full flavored tobacco used in cigars and in pipe blends. It has a large and dense cauliflower-like flower head of pink blossoms, and is quite showy. A good plant for the flower garden and also a good smoking tobacco. Usually air-cured.

Days to Maturity: 43-55
Spacing: 24-36 inches
Plant Height: 23-45 inches
Leaf Length: 9½-24 inches
Leaf Width: 10½-12½ inches
Leaf Count: 8-22

Comments:

ARS-GRIN
PI 405584
TI 1254
Yield: 2-2½ ounces of cured leaf per plant
Nicotine: 2.42%

Photos: ARS-GRIN, ARS-GRIN, ARS-GRIN

Oriental — Smyrna 9 — Oriental

Smyrna 9 is an Oriental Basma variety of the Izmir type. (Smyrna is the Ancient name of Izmir.) Usually sun-cured. Useful for cigarette and pipe blending. Closer spacing and minimal fertilizer use will produce smaller, more fragrant and more traditional Turkish leaf. Wider spacing and increased fertilization will produce much larger leaf that lacks its Oriental character.

Days to Maturity: 45-60
Spacing: 12-18 inches
Plant Height: 53½-75 inches
Leaf Length: 14½-16 inches
Leaf Width: 8-9 inches
Leaf Count: 18-27

Comments:

ARS-GRIN
PI 552414
TC 544
Yield: 2 ounces of cured leaf per plant
Nicotine:

Photos: ARS-GRIN, ARS-GRIN, ARS-GRIN

Oriental   Sultansko   Oriental

Sultansko is an heirloom oriental variety grown in Bulgaria. Can be sun-cured or air-cured. Useful for cigarette and pipe blending. Closer spacing and minimal fertilizer use will produce smaller, more fragrant and more traditional Oriental leaf. Wider spacing and increased fertilization will produce much larger leaf that lacks its Oriental character.

Days to Maturity: 36-47
Spacing: 12-16 inches
Plant Height: 31-37½ inches
Leaf Length: 14½-16½ inches
Leaf Width: 10 inches
Leaf Count: 13-16

Comments:

ARS-GRIN
PI 286828
TI 1387
Yield: 1-1½ ounces of cured leaf per plant
Nicotine: 1.16%

Photos: Northwood Seeds, ARS-GRIN

Oriental **Tasova** **Oriental**

Tasova is an Oriental variety of the Samsun group (heart-shaped leaf with a fringed petiole.) Tasova is 30 miles south of the port city of Samsun. *[ARS-GRIN incorrectly lists this accession as "Tasoua", as a result of a typing error in the original accession document.]* Tasova tobacco is quite similar to Samsun in its characteristics. Usually sun-cured. Useful for cigarette and pipe blending. Closer spacing and minimal fertilizer use will produce smaller, more fragrant and more traditional Turkish leaf. Wider spacing and increased fertilization will produce much larger leaf that lacks its Oriental character.

Days to Maturity: 56-77
Spacing: 12 inches
Plant Height: 42-59 inches
Leaf Length: 14-16 inches
Leaf Width: 9-10 inches
Leaf Count: 21-24

Comments:

ARS-GRIN
PI 494163
TI 1681
Yield:
Nicotine:

Photos: ARS-GRIN, ARS-GRIN, RCAG

Oriental Tekkekoy Oriental

Tekkekoy is an Oriental variety that appears to be more closely related to Basma-type tobaccos than Samsun, even though the Municipality of Tekkekoy is an eastern suburb of the port city of Samsun. Tekkekoy's leaf attachment (sessile) is similar to that of Basma, and its overall shape similar as well. Usually sun-cured. Useful for cigarette and pipe blending. Closer spacing and minimal fertilizer use will produce smaller, more fragrant and more traditional Turkish leaf. Wider spacing and increased fertilization will produce much larger leaf that lacks its Oriental character.

Days to Maturity: 65
Spacing: 6-12 inches
Plant Height: 84-96 inches
Leaf Length: 12-14 inches
Leaf Width: 5-6 inches
Leaf Count: 30-35

Comments:

Yield:
Nicotine:

Photos: Northwood Seeds

Oriental　　Tekne　　Oriental

Tekne is a large Hungarian variety. Air-cures to a reddish-brown. Can be air-cured or sun-cured. Useful for cigarette and pipe blending.

Days to Maturity: 21-41
Spacing: 24-36 inches
Plant Height: 30-84 inches
Leaf Length: 16½ inches
Leaf Width: 9½ inches
Leaf Count: 12-18

Comments:

ARS-GRIN
PI 286829
TI 1388
Yield: 1-1½ ounces of cured leaf per plant
Nicotine: 2.27%

Photos: ARS-GRIN, ARS-GRIN

Oriental — Trabzon — Oriental

Trabzon is an Oriental variety from the region of Turkey's Black Sea coast, east of Samsun. Trabzon is in the Samsun family, with heart- or spade-shaped leaves growing on a fringed petiole. It can be primed or stalk-cut. Usually sun-cured. Sun-cures to a light red-brown. Useful for cigarette and pipe blending. Closer spacing and minimal fertilizer use will produce smaller, more fragrant and more traditional Turkish leaf. Wider spacing and increased fertilization will produce much larger leaf that lacks its Oriental character. *(In the photos, the author has planted 25 plants in a 5'x6' bed.)*

[NOTE: ARS-GRIN accession PI 120513 appears to be a random, flue-cure variety from somewhere else, that happened to be found growing in a farmer's field near Trabzon in 1937. That accession is not Trabzon Oriental.]

Days to Maturity: 29-55
Spacing: 6-12 inches
Plant Height: 22-41 inches
Leaf Length: 11½-16 inches
Leaf Width: 6-8 inches
Leaf Count: 9-16

Home-grown Trabzon stalks hung to sun-cure.

Comments:

ARS-GRIN holds two similar accessions of Trabzon Oriental: *(photos are of accession a)*
a) PI 481862; b) PI 494164
a) TI 1649; b) TI 1682
Yield: ½-1 ounces of cured leaf per plant
Nicotine:

Photos: all RCAG

Oriental Turkish 1 Oriental

"Turkish 1" is one of nearly two dozen unnamed tobacco varieties collected from unidentified (by ARS-GRIN) locations in Turkey. Classed as Oriental. *[Since the plants in the ARS-GRIN photos are spaced considerably more widely than one might expect, the size measurements are likely much larger than when grown at typical, Turkish, close-spacing.]* Probably sun-cured. Useful for cigarette and pipe blending. Closer spacing and minimal fertilizer use will produce smaller, more fragrant and more traditional Turkish leaf. Wider spacing and increased fertilization will produce much larger leaf that lacks its Oriental character.

["Turkish 1" and "Turkish 2" are different varieties.]

This looks like an interesting plant, and a home-grower might produce something nice from it.

Days to Maturity: 42-55
Spacing: 6-12 inches
Plant Height: 31½-43½ inches
Leaf Length: 19-27 inches
Leaf Width: 11½-14 inches
Leaf Count: 15-17

Comments:

ARS-GRIN
PI 405566
TI 1235
Yield: 1-3 ounces of cured leaf per plant
Nicotine: 1.66%

Photos: ARS-GRIN, ARS-GRIN, ARS-GRIN

Oriental — Turkish 2 — Oriental

"Turkish 2" is one of nearly two dozen unnamed tobacco varieties collected from unidentified (by ARS-GRIN) locations in Turkey. Classed as Oriental. *[Since the plants in the ARS-GRIN photos are spaced considerably more widely than one might expect, the size measurement are likely much larger than when grown at typical, Turkish, close-spacing.]* Probably sun-cured. Useful for cigarette and pipe blending. Closer spacing and minimal fertilizer use will produce smaller, more fragrant and more traditional Turkish leaf. Wider spacing and increased fertilization will produce much larger leaf that lacks its Oriental character.

["Turkish 1" and "Turkish 2" are different varieties.] This looks like an interesting plant, and a home-grower might produce something nice from it.

Days to Maturity: 29-43
Spacing: 6-12 inches
Plant Height: 25-36 inches
Leaf Length: 15-16 inches
Leaf Width: 9-11½ inches
Leaf Count: 11-14

Comments:

ARS-GRIN
PI 405568
TI TI 1237
Yield: 1-2 ounces of cured leaf per plant
Nicotine: 1.77%

Photos: Northwood Seeds, ARS-GRIN, ARS-GRIN

Oriental — Variegata Samsun — Oriental

Variegata Samsun is a Samsun Oriental variety with a mutation that produces variegated leaves. Statistically, 25% of the plants will carry this mutation, even when seed is taken from a self pollinated variegated plant. The remaining 75% will develop into a normal looking Samsun. Variegation is due to the lack of chlorophyll production in certain areas of the leaf.

There is a particular cell membrane protease that is variably unstable, and its instability is likely the result of a recessive genetic trait. Reduction or lack of that protease in laminar cells inhibits chlorophyll production. So one can expect that no more than 25% of the self-pollinated offspring may be capable of exhibiting variegation. As shown in completely white burley leaf (Chillard's White Angel Leaf), the lack of chlorophyll in a particular leaf has no impact on subsequent color-curing or cured leaf quality.

Usually sun-cured. Useful for cigarette and pipe blending. Closer spacing and minimal fertilizer use will produce smaller, more fragrant and more traditional Turkish leaf. Wider spacing and increased fertilization will produce much larger leaf that lacks its Oriental character.

Days to Maturity: 50-70
Spacing: 12-16 inches
Plant Height: 42 inches
Leaf Length: 16-19 inches
Leaf Width: 11½-15 inches
Leaf Count: 18-20

Comments:

Yield: 1-2 ounces of cured leaf per plant
Nicotine:

Photos: Northwood Seeds, Northwood Seeds, Northwood Seeds

Oriental   Vavilov   Oriental

Vavilov: *[may or may not be Oriental]* Its leaf is spade-shaped and petiolate. The exact variety of this tobacco is unknown, as is the class. The leaf resembles the Samsun family of Orientals, but could also be of East Asian or Indonesian lineage. The seed is said to have originated from the collection of Nikolai Vavilov, a prominent Russian botanist and geneticist, best known for having identified the origins of the world's most cultivated plants. *[Vavilov's seed collection has over 200,000 specimens from around the world.]* This tobacco air cures easily, and sun cures to a light golden brown. Useful for cigarette and pipe blending.

Days to Maturity: 45-50
Spacing: 12-16 inches
Plant Height: 72 inches
Leaf Length: 10 inches
Leaf Width: 7 inches
Leaf Count: 28

Comments:

Yield:
Nicotine:

Photos: Northwood Seeds, Northwood Seeds

Oriental **White Flower (Cusco)** **Oriental**

White Flower (Cusco) is an heirloom Oriental tobacco from near Cusco, Peru, collected by Raymond Stadelman in 1936. The green foliage and abundant white flowers make it an attractive garden plant. Curing method uncertain, likely air-cured or sun-cured.

Days to Maturity: 42-84
Spacing: 12-16 inches
Plant Height: 24-48 inches
Leaf Length: 14-19½ inches
Leaf Width: 9½-12 inches
Leaf Count: 12-16

Comments:

ARS-GRIN
PI 116162
TI 722
Yield:
Nicotine: 1.28-2.99%

Photos: ARS-GRIN, ARS-GRIN, ARS-GRIN

Oriental — Xanthi-Yaka 18A — Oriental

Xanthi-Yaka 18A is an Oriental variety that typifies the finest Basma-type leaf grown on the slopes below the city of Xanthi, Greece, and is similar to the tobacco that was replanted in Genice (Yenidje) following its destruction by catastrophic floods in the late 19th century. *[Xanthi grown at higher elevations—on the steeper slopes above the city of Xanthi—is Xanthi-Djebel.]*

Usually sun-cured. Useful for cigarette and pipe blending. Closer spacing and minimal fertilizer use will produce smaller, more fragrant and more traditional Oriental leaf. Wider spacing and increased fertilization will produce much larger leaf that lacks its Oriental character. *[Xanthi-Yaka grown at 24 inch spacing will reach 48-60 inches in height, with much larger leaf, while that planted at 6-12 inches will grow to 30-36 inches, and produce delicate leaves similar to those in commercial Xanthi.]*

Days to Maturity: 42-45
Spacing: 6-12 inches
Plant Height: 36-48 inches
Leaf Length: 10-13½ inches
Leaf Width: 5-8 inches
Leaf Count: 17-23

Home-grown Xanthi-Yaka 18A strung to sun-cure

Comments:

ARS-GRIN
PI 552418
TC 552
Yield: ¾-1 ounces of cured leaf per plant
Nicotine:

Photos: RCAG, ARS-GRIN, ARS-GRIN, RCAG

Oriental — Xanthy — Oriental

"Xanthy" is a transliteration of "Xanthi" from Russian to English. This is the Oriental variety Xanthi, though lacking specifics. *[ARS-GRIN lists 9 accessions with the name Xanthi. Most are likely similar, if not identical.]* Xanthi is a Basma-type. Usually sun-cured. Useful for cigarette and pipe blending. Closer spacing and minimal fertilizer use will produce smaller, more fragrant and more traditional Oriental leaf. Wider spacing and increased fertilization will produce much larger leaf that lacks its Oriental character.

Days to Maturity: 42-50
Spacing: 6-12 inches
Plant Height: 36-48 inches
Leaf Length: 10-13½ inches
Leaf Width: 5-8 inches
Leaf Count: 17-23

Comments:

Yield: ¾-1 ounces of cured leaf per plant
Nicotine:

Photos: Northwood Seeds

Oriental — Yayladag — Oriental

Yayladag is a Turkish Oriental of the Basma type. The city of Yayladag is near the Mediterranean coast of the Levant, only about 30 miles north of the Syrian city of Latakia. Usually sun-cured. Useful for cigarette and pipe blending. Closer spacing and minimal fertilizer use will produce smaller, more fragrant and more traditional Turkish leaf. Wider spacing and increased fertilization will produce much larger leaf that lacks its Oriental character.

Days to Maturity: 10-45
Spacing: 6-12 inches
Plant Height: 34½-48 inches
Leaf Length: 16½-18 inches
Leaf Width: 8-10 inches
Leaf Count: 12-14

Comments:

ARS-GRIN
PI 481856
TI 1643
Yield: ~1 ounce of cured leaf per plant
Nicotine:

Photos: ARS-GRIN, ARS-GRIN, ARS-GRIN

Oriental — Yenidje — Oriental

Yenidje is the Oriental variety that is the result of replanting of the destroyed tobacco fields (from a catastrophic flood in the late 19th century) in Yenidje, or Genisea, Greece, with the Yaka type grown in Xanthi—a mere 6 miles up the river valley. It is a Basma type. It is said to be different today than Xanthi-Yaka. Usually sun-cured. Useful for cigarette and pipe blending. Closer spacing and minimal fertilizer use will produce smaller, more fragrant and more traditional Oriental leaf. Wider spacing and increased fertilization will produce much larger leaf that lacks its Oriental character.

[ARS-GRIN lists no accession identifiable as Yenidje or any of its many spellings. It is the author's suspicion that "Yenidje" is Xanthi-Yaka, and that "Yenidje" as a distinct tobacco variety is a famed myth from Balkan Sobranie Smoking Mixture marketing that spanned over decades.]

Days to Maturity: 42-65
Spacing: 6-12 inches
Plant Height: 36-48 inches
Leaf Length: 7-12 inches
Leaf Width: 5-8 inches
Leaf Count: 17-23

Comments:

Yield: ½-1 ounces of cured leaf per plant
Nicotine:

Photos: Northwood Seeds, Northwood Seeds

Ornamental — Affinis — Ornamental

Affinis is a synonym for *Nicotiana alata*, rather than a separate species. (As with most ornamental plants, numerous cultivars have been developed from *Nicotiana alata*.) It is a native of South America, from Brazil to northeastern Argentina.

Affinis grows to an average height of 4 feet. Blooms appear about 3 weeks after transplanting. It produces blossoms of various shades of pinks, pale purple, red, cream and occasionally blue, that open in late afternoon. It has many branching flower stems that grow to 3 feet long and have single blooms about 3 inches apart along the whole length of the stems and branches. They bloom profusely for the whole summer season, until frost arrives

Not for smoking or other tobacco use. *[N. alata roots produce nicotine and other alkaloids, but fail to transport most of the alkaloids to the leaves. As a result, the leaves will be more attractive to a greater variety of insect herbivores.]*

Synonyms:
Nicotiana alata
Nicotiana acutifolia
Nicotiana affinis
Nicotiana decurrens
Nicotiana persica
Nicotiana pseudodecurrens

Comments:

Photos: Northwood Seeds, Northwood Seeds

Ornamental Jasmine Ornamental

Jasmine tobacco is a cultivar of *Nicotiana alata*, rather than a separate species. (As with most ornamental plants, numerous cultivars have been developed from *Nicotiana alata*.) It is a native of South America, from Brazil to northeastern Argentina.

Jasmine is a fast-growing ornamental that can be planted in early spring. It starts blooming in only 3 weeks after transplant, and produces a profusion of sweet-smelling flowers that last all summer long. The flowers close during the day, and reopen in the late afternoon. Jasmine has a sweet fragrance that fills the evening air in the surrounding area. It is also attractive to Hummingbirds.

Not for smoking or other tobacco use. *[N. alata roots produce nicotine and other alkaloids, but fail to transport most of the alkaloids to the leaves. As a result, the leaves will be more attractive to a greater variety of insect herbivores.]*

Synonyms:
Nicotiana alata
Nicotiana acutifolia
Nicotiana affinis
Nicotiana decurrens
Nicotiana persica
Nicotiana pseudodecurrens

Comments:

Photos: Northwood Seeds, Northwood Seeds

Only the Lonely

Ornamental — **Ornamental**

"Only the Lonely" is a cultivar of *Nicotiana sylvestris*, rather than a separate species. It is a native of the Andes regions in Bolivia and Argentina, South America. It is thought to be one of the "parents" of *Nicotiana tabacum* (together with *N. tomentosa*).

Only The Lonely is an Ornamental. The long trumpet shaped, showy white flowers are attractive to bees and hummingbirds.

Not for smoking or other tobacco use. [*Nicotiana sylvestris* produces leaves that contain high levels assorted alkaloids which may cause physical symptoms if used like leaf from *N. tabacum*.]

Only the Lonely can reach 60 inches in height, with a rosette of leaves spreading to 48 inches.

Comments:

Photos: ARS-GRIN, ARS-GRIN

Ornamental — Sylvestris — Ornamental

Nicotiana sylvestris is also known as woodland tobacco. It is a native of the Andes regions in Bolivia and Argentina, South America. It is thought to be one of the "parents" of *Nicotiana tabacum* (together with *N. tomentosa*).

N. sylvestris is considered an Ornamental. The long trumpet shaped, showy white flowers are attractive to bees and hummingbirds.

Not for smoking or other tobacco use. [*Nicotiana sylvestris* produces leaves that contain high levels assorted alkaloids which may cause physical symptoms if used like leaf from N. tabacum.]

N. sylvestris can reach 60 inches in height, with a rosette of leaves spreading to 48 inches.

Comments:

Photos: ARS-GRIN, ARS-GRIN

Primitive — Bosikappal — Primitive

Bosikappal, from India, is classified as a primitive variety, indicating little evidence of agronomic selection or improvement. Air-cured leaves have a flavor described as sweet and slightly woody. Useful for cigarette and pipe blending.

Days to Maturity: 43-57
Spacing: 24-36 inches
Plant Height: 35-38½ inches
Leaf Length: 20½-24½ inches
Leaf Width: 5½-9 inches
Leaf Count: 13-18

Comments:

ARS-GRIN
PI 405634
TI 1358
Yield: 1-2½ ounces of cured leaf per plant
Nicotine: 2.58%

Photos: ARS-GRIN, ARS-GRIN, ARS-GRIN

Primitive — Chapeollo — Primitive

Chapeollo is a primitive variety from Honduras, collected for the USDA in 1936. Air-cures to a dark brown. Useful for cigarette, pipe blending and perhaps cigars and oral preparations.

Days to Maturity: 45-51
Spacing: 24-36 inches
Plant Height: 29-44½ inches
Leaf Length: 12-18½ inches
Leaf Width: 5-9½ inches
Leaf Count: 15

Comments:

ARS-GRIN
PI 114688
TI 675
Yield: ½-2½ ounces of cured leaf per plant
Nicotine: 2.37%

Photos: ARS-GRIN, ARS-GRIN, ARS-GRIN

Primitive — Chichicaste — Primitive

Chichicaste, a primitive variety, was collected in Honduras in 1936. Chichicaste is the name of a small village ~20 miles east of Danli. The same variety is know locally in Cuba as "Burro." Useful for full-flavored cigar filler.

Days to Maturity: 40-60
Spacing: 24-36 inches
Plant Height: 42½-65 inches
Leaf Length: 15-19 inches
Leaf Width: 7-10 inches
Leaf Count: 14-19

Comments:

ARS-GRIN
PI 116087
TI 712
Yield: 1½-2½ ounces of cured leaf per plant
Nicotine: 2.4%

Photos: ARS-GRIN, RCAG, RCAG

Cuba 4 — Primitive

Cuba 4 (Actually named merely, "Cuba", and listed as TI 4) had been held by the Tobacco Laboratory, Plant Genetics and Germplasm Institute, Beltsville, Maryland for an undisclosed length of time. It was sent from there to ARS-GRIN in 1975. Its original source (and date) are not available. It is classed as a primitive, though the leaf shape, nicotine and productivity are typical for cigar filler. Secondary vein angles and a rugose leaf would appear to limit its use as cigar binder or wrapper. This is essentially a mystery variety. May also be useful for cigarette and pipe blending. Suitable for air-curing.

Days to Maturity:
Spacing: 24-36 inches
Plant Height: 42-49 inches
Leaf Length: 13½-16 inches
Leaf Width: 7½-9½ inches
Leaf Count: 15-17

Comments:

ARS-GRIN
PI 404935
TI 4
Yield: ~2 ounces of cured leaf per plant
Nicotine: 2.71%

Photos: ARS-GRIN, ARS-GRIN, ARS-GRIN

Primitive — Daule — Primitive

Daule is a native tobacco variety from Ecuador. Both accessions were by Raymond Stadelman in 1936, in Ecuador. Accession a) was collected by him along the Daule River, while accession b) was presented to him by a tobacco official 3 weeks later, in Guayaquil. Accession a) is classed as "cigar filler", while accession b) is classed as a "primitive." In the full photos, both show some variability in height and leaf size. Both display the same secondary vein angle and nearly identical blossoms. *[The author suspects the two accessions are variants of the same variety, despite somewhat differing size measurements.]* Air cures to a light brown.

Days to Maturity: a) 57-76; b) 34-47
Spacing: 24-36 inches
Plant Height: a) 63-68; b) 32½-34? inches
Leaf Length: a) 10-13; b) 15¾-19 inches
Leaf Width: a) 10-13; b) 7½-8¼ inches
Leaf Count: a) 18-20; b)10-13

Leaf b) ~13 inches

Comments:

ARS-GRIN
a) PI 114369; b) PI 115102
a) TI 588; b) TI 691
Yield: a) 2¾; b) 1-1½ ounces of cured leaf per plant
Nicotine: a) 1.99%; b) 2.16%

Photos: ARS-GRIN, ARS-GRIN, ARS-GRIN

Primitive   **Guácharo**   **Primitive**

Guácharo is a primitive tobacco variety, native to Venezuela. [classed by ARS-GRIN as cigar filler] It was collected by Raymond Stadelman in 1936, at an elevation of about 5000 feet. Though much more compact, Guácharo resembles the other characteristics and finished leaf quality of Bolivia Criollo Black, Tobacco Negro and other similar varieties native to the Andes highlands (e.g. Flojo). Useful for cigar filler. Also cooks into a rich Cavendish, for pipe blending.

Days to Maturity: 51-81
Spacing: 24-36 inches
Plant Height: 33½-52 inches
Leaf Length: 20-21½ inches
Leaf Width: 6½-9½ inches
Leaf Count: 15-27

Comments:

ARS-GRIN
PI 118177
TI 899
Yield: 2½-3 ounces of cured leaf per plant
Nicotine: 1.86%

Photos: ARS-GRIN, ARS-GRIN, RCAG

Primitive   # Hyang Cho   **Primitive**

Hyang Cho is a primitive variety originally from South Korea. When ripe, the leaves become a dappled green and yellow and air cure to a rich medium brown. Useful for pipe blending and perhaps oral preparations.

Days to Maturity: 33-45
Spacing: 24 inches
Plant Height: 36-48 inches
Leaf Length: 9½-18 inches
Leaf Width: 5-10½ inches
Leaf Count: 2-12

Comments:

ARS-GRIN
PI 405595
TI 1275
Yield: ½-2 ounces of cured leaf per plant
Nicotine: 5.85%

Photos: Northwood Seeds, Northwood Seeds, ARS-GRIN

Primitive — Iztepeque — Primitive

Iztepeque is a primitive variety (classed as "Oriental" by ARS-GRIN!) collected from Costa Rica in 1936. *["Seed collected from off type plant in field of Itztepeque that had white and pink varigated flowers."]* The leaves air-cure to a light brown. It has a mild flavor, and is useful for pipe blending, or as cigar filler.

Days to Maturity: 33-53
Spacing: 24-36 inches
Plant Height: 58 inches
Leaf Length: 14½-18 inches
Leaf Width: 5-10 inches
Leaf Count: 14-19

Comments:

ARS-GRIN
PI 114370
TI 589
Yield: 1-2 ounces of cured leaf per plant
Nicotine: 3.75%

Photos: RCAG, ARS-GRIN, RCAG

Little Cuba

Primitive

Little Cuba, classed by ARS-GRIN as "primitive," is a small plant that matures early. Its use in cigars is limited to filler. May serve to broaden the flavor profile of pipe blends.

Days to Maturity: 37-38
Spacing: 24 inches
Plant Height: 19½-29 inches
Leaf Length: 13-15 inches
Leaf Width: 5½-9 inches
Leaf Count: 8-14

Comments:

ARS-GRIN
PI 405669
TI 1454
Yield: ½-2 ounces of cured leaf per plant
Nicotine: 1.39%

Photos: Northwood Seeds, ARS-GRIN, ARS-GRIN

Primitive — Mopan Mayan — Primitive

Mopan Mayan is an heirloom tobacco grown in Guatemala by the Mopan Maya natives, direct descendants of the ancient Maya. (The Mopan River originates in the highlands of northeastern Guatemala, and descends into western Belize.) It is a primitive plant. Air-cures to a light brown. Useful for cigarette, pipe blending and cigar filler.

Days to Maturity: 47-78
Spacing: 24-36 inches
Plant Height: 60 inches
Leaf Length: 14-16 inches
Leaf Width: 6-12 inches
Leaf Count: 28

Comments:

Yield:
Nicotine: 2.8%

Photos: Northwood Seeds, Northwood Seeds

Mostrenco

Primitive

Mostrenco ("monstrosity") is a cultivated variety of tobacco collected by W.A. Archer in Encarnación de Díaz, Jalisco, Mexico, in 1935. It is classed as primitive. The leaves air cure to a dark brown. Useful for cigarette and pipe blending.

Days to Maturity: 40-54
Spacing: 24-36 inches
Plant Height: 37½-60 inches
Leaf Length: 19½-22 inches
Leaf Width: 7½-16 inches
Leaf Count: 14-16

Comments:

ARS-GRIN
PI 114574
TI 658
Yield: 1¼-2½ ounces of cured leaf per plant
Nicotine: 2.11%

Photos: ARS-GRIN, Northwood Seeds, ARS-GRIN

Mountain Pima

Primitive — **Primitive**

Mountain Pima is a primitive tobacco variety that closely resembles Little Dutch in its appearance, though its finished leaf quality is coarser. Mountain Pima resembles Papante even more closely. It is unclear if the name, "Mountain Pima," actually relates to the Native tribal, Mountain Pima people (or the Taramil 'O'Odham). This variety has been incorrectly described and sold as *Nicotiana rustica*. Leaves air-cure to a medium brown. Useful for cigarette and pipe blending.

Days to Maturity: 55
Spacing: 24-36 inches
Plant Height: 28 inches
Leaf Length: 24 inches
Leaf Width: 9 inches
Leaf Count: 16

Comments:

Yield:
Nicotine:

Photos: Northwood Seeds, RCAG, RCAG

Primitive — Okinawa — Primitive

Okinawa is classed by ARS-GRIN as "primitive", suggesting little to no agronomic development. But it was cultivated in Japan, where it was developed. The leaves have a fringed petiole, like Samsun. Creamy white blossom. It is resistant to tropical root knot nematodes (Meloidogyne javanica). The leaves air-cure a light brown. Traditional curing methods are unclear. Useful for cigarette, pipe blending and perhaps cigar filler.

Days to Maturity: 65-70
Spacing: 24-36 inches
Plant Height: 84 inches
Leaf Length: 12-20 inches
Leaf Width: 9-16 inches
Leaf Count: ~14-18

Comments:

Yield:
Nicotine:

Photos: ARS-GRIN, Northwood Seeds, Northwood Seeds

Papante

Primitive — *Primitive*

Papante is a primitive variety that likely comes from southeastern area of the Mexican state of Sonora. A specimen is on display at the Conservation Center in Tucson, AZ. The plant's general appearance resembles that of both Little Dutch and Mountain Pima, though the leaf is a darker green. It has been incorrectly listed and sold as *Nicotiana rustica*. Air-cures to a soft, light brown. Useful for cigarette, pipe blending and cigar filler. It's relatively square secondary vein angle allows it to be used for cigar wrapper or binder.

Days to Maturity: 52-60
Spacing: 24-36 inches
Plant Height: 40-48 inches
Leaf Length: 20-21 inches
Leaf Width: 10 inches
Leaf Count: 19

Home-grown Papante wrapper

Comments:

Yield:
Nicotine:

Photos: all RCAG

Primitive — Pretinho — Primitive

Pretinho is a cultivated, native, heirloom tobacco from the state of Para, in northern Brazil. (Accession received in 1935, and classed as primitive.) Air-cured. It is a good cigar filler, with a unique aroma and earthy flavor. May also be useful for cigarette and pipe blending.

Days to Maturity: 40-49
Spacing: 24-36 inches
Plant Height: 48-53 inches
Leaf Length: 15½-18½ inches
Leaf Width: 6½-10 inches
Leaf Count: 14-15

Comments:

ARS-GRIN
PI 110680
TI 171
Yield: 1-1½ ounces of cured leaf per plant
Nicotine: 1.81%

Photos: ARS-GRIN, ARS-GRIN, Northwood Seeds

| Primitive | Tabaco Colorado | Primitive |

Tabaco Colorado is a primitive variety from Mexico. ARS-GRIN holds 3 accessions of Tabaco Colorado, each collected by W.A. Archer during the summer of 1936, in the boundary area between the Mexican states of Veracruz and Oaxaca. Photos of the entire plants, blossoms and leaf shape appear nearly identical. *[The author suspects that these three accessions all represent examples of the same variety.]* Air-cured. Useful for cigarette and pipe blending, as well as cigar filler.

Photos of the plant and blossoms shown are of accession a) PI 116626, TI 748

Days to Maturity: ~56
Spacing: 24-36 inches
Plant Height: a) 68; b) 48 ; c) 48 inches
Leaf Length: a) 14-20; b) 14-20; c) 8-14 inches
Leaf Width: a) 4-6; b) 6-9; c) 4-6 inches
Leaf Count: 14-18

Comments:

ARS-GRIN (3 accessions)
a) PI 116626; b) PI 116628; c) PI 116629
a) TI 748; b) TI 750; c) TI 751
Yield:
Nicotine:

Photos: ARS-GRIN, ARS-GRIN, ARS-GRIN

Primitive — Tabasqueño Prieto — Primitive

Tabasqueño Prieto is a primitive Mexican tobacco collected by W.A. Archer, in San Andres Tuxtla, Veracruz, 1936. It is not as productive as more improved varieties, but is an interesting and authentic tobacco, with a rich aroma. Air-cured. (It does *not* flue-cure gracefully.) Useful as cigar filler, and as an ingredient in cigarette and pipe blends.

Days to Maturity: 38-53
Spacing: 24-36 inches
Plant Height: 41-58 inches
Leaf Length: 14-18 inches
Leaf Width: 6-9 inches
Leaf Count: 12-19

Comments:

ARS-GRIN
PI 114401
TI 627
Yield: 1-1½ ounces of cured leaf per plant
Nicotine: 3.60%

Photos: ARS-GRIN, ARS-GRIN, RCAG

Primitive   Yumbo   Primitive

Yumbo is a primitive variety of tobacco. The origin of the varietal name, "Yumbo," is unclear. The ancient Yumbo trading culture existed in the area of Ecuador, just west of Quito, during pre-Inca times, and spread regionally through the Yumbo's trading networks. Two hundred miles north, there is a city of Yumbo, Colombia. *[After the Inca conquests, immediately followed by the Spanish conquest and its accompaniment of multiple scourges of European diseases, the Yumbo people are likely now extinct.]* The tobacco varietal going by that name is probably unrelated to tobacco that the Yumbo people may once have cultivated, traded and used.

Sun-cured or air-cured. Useful for cigarette and pipe blending, and possibly as a cigar filler ingredient.

Days to Maturity: 45-77
Spacing: 24-36 inches
Plant Height: 36-40 inches
Leaf Length: 14-16½ inches
Leaf Width: 9-12 inches
Leaf Count: 12-16

Comments:

Yield:
Nicotine: 1.80%

Photos: Northwood Seeds, Northwood Seeds

Aztec

N. rustica

Aztec is a variety of *Nicotiana rustica*. Aztec Rustica —Rapi Nui strain, said to be from Easter Island. *Nicotiana rustica* was actively cultivated in Central and North America for thousands of years. Varieties of it were also propagated into South America. It grows with abundant bright yellow flowers that are attractive to bees and hummingbirds. Flowering lasts up to two months. Leaves air-cure to a medium-to-dark brown, and produce a very mild flavored smoke. Grows well in cool climates and tolerates frost. As with all *N. rustica* varieties, the leaves should be allowed to yellow on the plant, prior to harvesting, to insure thorough color-curing. Useful for cigarette and pipe blending.

Days to Maturity: ~40
Spacing: 24-36 inches
Plant Height: ~30 inches
Leaf Length: 9½ inches
Leaf Width: 6 inches
Leaf Count: 8

Comments:

Yield:
Nicotine:

Photos: Northwood Seeds, Northwood Seeds

N. rustica — Brasilia 7 — N. rustica

Brasilia 7 is a variety of *Nicotiana rustica*. As with all *N. rustica* varieties (actively cultivated for thousands of years in Central and North America), the leaves should be allowed to yellow on the plant, prior to harvesting, to insure thorough color-curing. *N. rustica* suckers prolifically. You can remove the suckers, to get larger primary leaf, or simply allow the suckers to grow, and harvest a larger number of smaller leaves. Useful for cigarette and pipe blending—in moderation. Most *N. rustica* varieties contain higher levels of nicotine than most *N. tabacum* varieties..

Days to Maturity: ~35-45
Spacing: 24-36 inches
Plant Height: 24-30 inches
Leaf Length: 8½ inches
Leaf Width: 8 inches
Leaf Count: 6-8

Comments:
ARS-GRIN (3 historical accessions listed, but no data)
PI 149054
PI 147903
PI 146296
[in 1944, all were also identified as "Aztec tobacco"]
Yield:
Nicotine:

N. rustica | **Hasenkeyf** | *N. rustica*

Hasankeyf is a "high yielding" variety of *Nicotiana rustica* used for making Turkish "Shag." Leaf is dark green and thick. As with all *N. rustica* varieties (actively cultivated for thousands of years in Central and North America), the leaves should be allowed to yellow on the plant, prior to harvesting, to insure thorough color-curing. *N. rustica* suckers prolifically. You can remove the suckers, to get larger primary leaf, or simply allow the suckers to grow, and harvest a larger number of smaller leaves. Useful for cigarette and pipe blending—in moderation. Most *N. rustica* varieties contain higher levels of nicotine than most *N. tabacum* varieties.

Days to Maturity: ~35-40
Spacing: 24-36 inches
Plant Height: ? inches
Leaf Length: 10 inches
Leaf Width: 6 inches
Leaf Count: 8-12

Comments:

Yield:
Nicotine: ~5%

N. rustica — Isleta Pueblo — N. rustica

Isleta Pueblo is a *Nicotiana rustica* variety believed to have originated in New Mexico. Leaf is dark green and thick. As with all *N. rustica* varieties (actively cultivated for thousands of years in Central and North America), the leaves should be allowed to yellow on the plant, prior to harvesting, to insure thorough color-curing. *N. rustica* suckers prolifically. You can remove the suckers, to get larger primary leaf, or simply allow the suckers to grow, and harvest a larger number of smaller leaves. Useful for cigarette and pipe blending—in moderation. Most *N. rustica* varieties contain higher levels of nicotine than most *N. tabacum* varieties. Air-cures to a medium brown.

Days to Maturity: 35-50
Spacing: 24-36 inches
Plant Height: 48-60 inches
Leaf Length: ~9 inches
Leaf Width: ~6 inches
Leaf Count: 12-14

Comments:

Yield:
Nicotine:

Photos: Northwood Seeds, Northwood Seeds

Karabaglar Rustica

N. rustica *N. rustica*

Karabaglar Rustica is a *Nicotiana rustica* variety collected in a field near Karabaglar, Turkey. Leaf is dark green and thick. As with all *N. rustica* varieties (actively cultivated for thousands of years in Central and North America), the leaves should be allowed to yellow on the plant, prior to harvesting, to insure thorough color-curing. *N. rustica* suckers prolifically. You can remove the suckers, to get larger primary leaf, or simply allow the suckers to grow, and harvest a larger number of smaller leaves. Useful for cigarette and pipe blending—in moderation. Most *N. rustica* varieties contain higher levels of nicotine than most *N. tabacum* varieties. Air-cures to a medium brown.

Days to Maturity:
Spacing: 24-36 inches
Plant Height: 30 inches
Leaf Length: 9 inches
Leaf Width: 6 inches
Leaf Count: 8-12

[Not to be confused with Izmir-Karabaglar]

Comments:

ARS-GRIN
PI 481867
TR 77
TI 1655
Yield:
Nicotine:

Photos: Northwood Seeds, Northwood Seeds

Mohawk

N. rustica

Mohawk is a *Nicotiana rustica* variety cultivated as a ceremonial tobacco by the tribes of the Haudenosaunee Confederacy, located in northeastern New York State. Leaf is dark green and thick. As with all *N. rustica* varieties (actively cultivated for thousands of years in Central and North America), the leaves should be allowed to yellow on the plant, prior to harvesting, to insure thorough color-curing. *N. rustica* suckers prolifically. You can remove the suckers, to get larger primary leaf, or simply allow the suckers to grow, and harvest a larger number of smaller leaves. Useful for cigarette and pipe blending—in moderation. Most *N. rustica* varieties contain higher levels of nicotine than most *N. tabacum* varieties. Air-cures to a medium brown.

Days to Maturity: 30-40
Spacing: 24-36 inches
Plant Height: 24-36 inches
Leaf Length: 10-12 inches
Leaf Width: 6-8 inches
Leaf Count: 8-12

Comments:

Yield:
Nicotine:

Photos: @billy (FTT), @billy (FTT), Daniel F. Taylor

Punche

N. rustica

N. rustica

Punche is a *Nicotiana rustica* variety. Leaf is dark green and thick. As with all *N. rustica* varieties (actively cultivated for thousands of years in Central and North America), the leaves should be allowed to yellow on the plant, prior to harvesting, to insure thorough color-curing. *N. rustica* suckers prolifically. You can remove the suckers, to get larger primary leaf, or simply allow the suckers to grow, and harvest a larger number of smaller leaves. Useful for cigarette and pipe blending—in moderation. Most *N. rustica* varieties contain higher levels of nicotine than most *N. tabacum* varieties. Air-cures to a medium brown.

Days to Maturity: 35
Spacing: 24-36 inches
Plant Height: ~24 inches
Leaf Length: 8-10 inches
Leaf Width: 4-6 inches
Leaf Count: 10-15

Comments:

Yield:
Nicotine:

Photos: Northwood Seeds, Northwood Seeds

| *N. rustica* | **Sacred Cornplanter** | *N. rustica* |

Sacred Cornplanter is a *Nicotiana rustica* variety cultivated as a ceremonial tobacco by Cornplanter, a war chief and diplomat of the Seneca tribe (of the Haudenosaunee Confederacy). The Seneca were located in northwestern New York State. Leaf is dark green and thick. As with all *N. rustica* varieties (actively cultivated for thousands of years in Central and North America), the leaves should be allowed to yellow on the plant, prior to harvesting, to insure thorough color-curing. *N. rustica* suckers prolifically. You can remove the suckers, to get larger primary leaf, or simply allow the suckers to grow, and harvest a larger number of smaller leaves. Useful for cigarette and pipe blending—in moderation. Most *N. rustica* varieties contain higher levels of nicotine than most *N. tabacum* varieties. Air-cures to a medium brown.

Days to Maturity: 57
Spacing: 24-36 inches
Plant Height: 35 inches
Leaf Length: 14 inches
Leaf Width: 10 inches
Leaf Count: 21

Curious Provenance:
During the early 20th century, 20+ year old seed at a museum display honoring Cornplanter was successfully germinated, to save this ceremonial variety.

Comments:

Yield:
Nicotine:

Photos: all RCAG

Sacred Wyandot

N. rustica

Sacred Wyandot (or Wyandotte) is a *Nicotiana rustica* variety cultivated as a ceremonial tobacco by the people of the Huron Confederacy (on the north shore of Lake Ontario), which was on the losing end of the wars with the Iroquois (Haudenosaunee) Confederacy during the mid 17th century. Leaf is dark green and thick. As with all *N. rustica* varieties (actively cultivated for thousands of years in Central and North America), the leaves should be allowed to yellow on the plant, prior to harvesting, to insure thorough color-curing. *N. rustica* suckers prolifically. You can remove the suckers, to get larger primary leaf, or simply allow the suckers to grow, and harvest a larger number of smaller leaves. Useful for cigarette and pipe blending—in moderation. Most *N. rustica* varieties contain higher levels of nicotine than most *N. tabacum* varieties. Air-cures to a medium brown.

Days to Maturity: ~35
Spacing: 24-36 inches
Plant Height: ~30 inches
Leaf Length: ~10-12 inches
Leaf Width: ~6-8 inches
Leaf Count: ~12-16

Comments:

Yield:
Nicotine:

Photos: Northwood Seeds, Northwood Seeds

N. rustica   Shtambur   N. rustica

Shtambur is a fast maturing variety of *Nicotiana rustica*. After beginning to bloom, it continues growing for another month, becoming a bushy plant. Leaf is dark green and thick. As with all *N. rustica* varieties (actively cultivated for thousands of years in Central and North America), the leaves should be allowed to yellow on the plant, prior to harvesting, to insure thorough color-curing. *N. rustica* suckers prolifically. You can remove the suckers, to get larger primary leaf, or simply allow the suckers to grow, and harvest a larger number of smaller leaves. Useful for cigarette and pipe blending—in moderation. Most *N. rustica* varieties contain higher levels of nicotine than most *N. tabacum* varieties. Air-cures to a medium brown.

Days to Maturity: ~30-35
Spacing: 24-36 inches
Plant Height: ~24-30 inches
Leaf Length: ~10-12 inches
Leaf Width: ~6-8 inches
Leaf Count: ~12-16

Comments:

Yield:
Nicotine:

Photos: Northwood Seeds

Sorotooskaia

N. rustica

Sorotooskaia is a variety of *Nicotiana rustica*. Leaf is dark green and thick. As with all *N. rustica* varieties (actively cultivated for thousands of years in Central and North America), the leaves should be allowed to yellow on the plant, prior to harvesting, to insure thorough color-curing. *N. rustica* suckers prolifically. You can remove the suckers, to get larger primary leaf, or simply allow the suckers to grow, and harvest a larger number of smaller leaves. Useful for cigarette and pipe blending—in moderation. Most *N. rustica* varieties contain higher levels of nicotine than most *N. tabacum* varieties. Air-cures to a medium brown.

Days to Maturity: ?
Spacing: 24-36 inches
Plant Height: ? inches
Leaf Length: ? inches
Leaf Width: ? inches
Leaf Count: ?

Comments:

Yield: ounces of cured leaf per plant
Nicotine:

Photos: Northwood Seeds, Northwood Seeds

N. rustica — Yellow 109 — *N. rustica*

Yellow 109 is a variety of *Nicotiana rustica* from the former Soviet Union. Leaves yellow on the tips and edges at they ripen. Nicotine ranges from 6% - 9% depending on soil type and fertilization. Leaf is dark green and thick. As with all N. rustica varieties (actively cultivated for thousands of years in Central and North America), the leaves should be allowed to yellow on the plant, prior to harvesting, to insure thorough color-curing. N. rustica suckers prolifically. You can remove the suckers, to get larger primary leaf, or simply allow the suckers to grow, and harvest a larger number of smaller leaves. Useful for cigarette and pipe blending—in moderation. Most N. rustica varieties contain higher levels of nicotine than most N. tabacum varieties. Air-cures to a medium brown.

Days to Maturity: 35
Spacing: 24-36 inches
Plant Height: 30 inches
Leaf Length: 8-10 inches
Leaf Width: 4-5 inches
Leaf Count: ~10-14

Comments:

ARS-GRIN
PI 499185
TR 27
Yield:
Nicotine:

Photos: ARS-GRIN, ARS-GRIN

Wild   Clevelandii   Wild

Nicotiana clevelandii is a wild tobacco found in the arid regions of the Southwestern United States. *N. Clevelandii* was cultivated by Native Americans in the western states, along with the more widespread *N. Quadravalvis*. It is very hardy and drought tolerant. Blooms appear about 3 weeks after transplanting. It continues to grow and produce beautiful trumpet shaped white flowers throughout the summer with occasional watering.

Days to Maturity: 27-30
Spacing: 12-16 inches
Plant Height: ? inches
Leaf Length: ? inches
Leaf Width: ? inches
Leaf Count: 8-14

Comments:

ARS-GRIN (variant A. Gray)
PI 555491
TW 30
Yield:
Nicotine: 6.2%

Photos: Northwood Seeds, Northwood Seeds, Northwood Seeds

Wild **Quadrivalvis** **Wild**

Nicotiana quadrivalvis is a species of wild tobacco native to the western United States, where it grows in many habitats. It is a bushy, sprawling, annual herb. *N. quadrivalvis* was cultivated by indigenous peoples on the west coast of North America, and into the western plains.

*[This is the tobacco discussed in **Buffalo Bird Woman's Garden As Recounted by Maxi'diwiac (Buffalo Bird Woman) (ca.1839-1932) of the Hidatsa Indian Tribe**, published in 1917.]*

Days to Maturity: ~25
Spacing: 12-16 inches
Plant Height: ~60 inches
Leaf Length: 5-6 inches
Leaf Width: 1-2 inches
Leaf Count: ~10-16

Comments:

ARS-GRIN (variant Pursh)
PI 555485
TW 18
Yield:
Nicotine: 7.3%

Photos: Northwood Seeds, ARS-GRIN, Northwood Seeds

Unclassified Bravyi 200 Unclassified

Bravyi 200 is an unclassified western Ukrainian variety, created by hybridizing a burley with a flue-cure variety. Said to have "good disease resistance." The plants grow in an upright, columnar form, with light green upturned leaves. The leaves do not change color when maturing. Suckering is very low. Leaves cure easily to a light golden brown, producing a medium strength tobacco. Bravyi 200 may primed or stalk-cured. Leaves ripen as blooming begins. Usual curing method is unclear. Most suitable for cigarette and pipe blending.

Days to Maturity: 60-65
Spacing: 24-36 inches
Plant Height: 42-84 inches
Leaf Length: 23½-26 inches
Leaf Width: 12-14 inches
Leaf Count: 22-25

Comments:

Yield:
Nicotine: 4.00%

Photos: Northwood Seeds

Unclassified Perique Unclassified

Perique is a variety of tobacco grown in Saint James Parish, Louisiana, and is used for making pressure-cured "Perique" there. The plant variety is likely derived from a now-lost variety of "red" burley, though the appearance alone of the mature plant strongly resembles the flue-cured variety, Hickory Pryor. The air-cured leaf quality clearly differs from that of either burley or flue-cured. *[The variety is incorrectly classed by ARS-GRIN as an Oriental, which it clearly is not. The author has chosen to consider the Perique variety as "unclassified", rather than to perpetuate that error.]*

Three definitions of "perique":
1) A perique is a compressed **bundle** of any tobacco.
2) **Commercial perique** is the perique variety that has been pressure-cured anaerobically.
3) The perique, anaerobic pressure-curing **process** can be used with any tobacco variety to make "perique."

Days to Maturity: 53-60
Spacing: 24-36 inches
Plant Height: 48-63 inches
Leaf Length: 19-28 inches
Leaf Width: 8½-13½ inches
Leaf Count: 17-22

Comments:

ARS-GRIN
PI 552742
TC 556
Yield: 1½-2 ounces of cured leaf per plant
Nicotine:

Photos: Northwood Seeds, Northwood Seeds, RCAG

| Unclassified | **Red Russian** | Unclassified |

Red Russian is an unclassified *Nicotiana tabacum* variety (dating back to before 1906). It has dark green leaves, and produces a reasonable yield of tobacco leaf. Its most striking feature is its large magenta flowers. Leaf air-cures to a light reddish-tan. Early 20th century studies of what has been identified as "Red Russian" (prior to its ARS-GRIN accession in 1939) conflated it with other varieties that display deep red blossoms. Little has been documented on its tobacco uses.

Days to Maturity: ~49
Spacing: 24-36 inches
Plant Height: 36-48 inches
Leaf Length: 14-19½ inches
Leaf Width: 9½-12 inches
Leaf Count: ~14-16

Comments:

ARS-GRIN
PI *none*
TC 588
Yield:
Nicotine:

Photos: Northwood Seeds, ARS-GRIN, ARS-GRIN

Unclassified   **Silver River**   **Unclassified**

Silver River is an unclassified variety of *Nicotiana tabacum*. It is unclassified, because it originated from an old seed packet, labeled "Silver River, wild," in an old, Ohio farmer's desk drawer. Nothing is known about its history. The leaves are easy to air-cure to a light brown. It produces a medium flavored, mild smoke. Some growers report a slight mint or menthol taste, while others do not. *[The author detects an unidentified terpene in the cured and aged leaf. The growth habit of Silver River closely resembles that of tobacco varieties native to the high plains of the Andes (e.g. Flojo, Guácharo, Bolivia Criollo Black), all of which taste of a similar terpene. By grower reports, that terpene varies with fertilization and year.]*

Days to Maturity: 75-95
Spacing: 24-36 inches
Plant Height: 84 inches
Leaf Length: 30-36 inches
Leaf Width: 12-20 inches
Leaf Count: 20-30

[There are also South American flue-cure varieties that have similar growth and aroma profiles, such as Amarello Rio Grande do Sul, from Uruguay. Silver River reportedly flue-cures well.]

Comments:

Yield:
Nicotine:

Photos: Northwood Seeds, Northwood Seeds.

Appendix: Spacing Oriental Varieties

[guidance provided by Emre Öztürk]

Variety	Space between two rows (cm / inch)	Space between plants in a row (cm / inch)
Aegean (İzmir)	40 / 15.7	5-10 / 2-3.9
Basma, Gümüşhacıköy, Xanthi	40 / 15.7	15 / 5.9
Black Sea (Karadeniz)	40 / 15.7	20 / 7.9
East - Southeast (Doğu-Güneydoğu)	50 / 19.7	20 / 7.9
Virginia - Burley	100 / 34.9	80 / 31.5
Tömbeki (Tombac)	100 / 34.9	80 / 31.5
Hasankeyf (*N. rustica*)	80 / 31.5	40 / 15.7

Plant spacing in the field

Variety	Width cm (inch)	Length cm (inch)	Descriptive
İzmir	5-7 (2-2.8)	5-12 (2-4.7)	Small - Moderately medium
Düzce	5-7.5 (2-3)	10-15 (3.9-5.9)	Moderately small - Medium
Trabzon	15-20 (5.9-7.9)	20-50 (7.9-19.7)	Large
Samsun Maden	3.5-5.5 (1.4-2.2)	7-17 (2.8-6.7)	Small
Bursa	6.5-10 (2.6-3.9)	10-15 (3.9-5.9)	Moderately small - Medium
Agonya – Balıkesir	8.5-14.5 (3.3- 5.7)	15-25 (5.9-9.8)	Medium - Moderately small
Taşova	6-12 (2.4-4.7)	12-20 (4.7-7.9)	Medium
Samsun Canik	3-4 (1.2-1.6)	7-12 (2.8-4.7)	Small
Bitlis	4.5-11.5 (1.8-4.5)	15-25 (5.9-9.8)	Medium
Gümüşhacıköy - Xanthi	2.5-5.5 (1-2.2)	3-6.5 (1.2-2.6)	Small
Yayladağ	8-10 (3.1-3.9)	15-25 (5.9-9.8)	Medium - Moderately Large
Adıyaman - Çelikhan	6.5-12 (2.6-4.7)	20-32 (7.9-12.6)	Medium - Moderately Large
Bucak	12-15 (4.7-5.9)	35-40 (13.8-15.7)	Large

Derirable leaf sizes for typical Orientals

Tobacco Plant Varieties for Home Growers

Adiyaman	Oriental	196	Coker 213	Bright	28
Adonis	Dark	170	Coker 371	Bright	29
Affinis	Ornamental	255	Colombian Garcia	Cigar	107
African Red	Bright	19	Comstock Spanish	Cigar	108
Ahus	Cigar	100	Connecticut 49	Cigar	109
Ainaro	Dark	171	Connecticut Broadleaf	Cigar	110
Alma Ata 315	Oriental	197	Connecticut Shade	Cigar	111
Amarello Rio Grande	Cigar	101	Coroja (Cuba)	Cigar	112
Amarillo Parado	Bight	102	Corojo (Honduras)	Cigar	113
American 14	Oriental	199	Corojo 99 (Cuba)	Cigar	114
American 26	Oriental	200	Costello Negro	Bright	30
American 3	Oriental	198	Crimean	Bright	31
American 572	Oriental	202	Criollo (Cuba)	Cigar	115
American 63	Oriental	201	Cuba 4	Primitive	262
Anatolian	Oriental	203	Criollo 98 (Cuba)	Cigar	116
Awa	Bright	20	Daule	Primitive	263
Aztec	Rustica	277	Delgold	Bright	32
Bafra	Oriental	204	Diamantina	Cigar	117
Bahia	Cigar	205	Dixie Bright 27	Bright	33
Baiano	Oriental	206	Dixie Shade	Cigar	118
Baldío Vera	Burley	72	Djebel 174	Oriental	213
Balikesir	Oriental	207	Dukat Crimean	Bright	214
Bamboo Shoot	Bright	21	Düzce	Oriental	215
Banana Leaf	Bright	22	Ege	Oriental	216
Basma	Oriental	208	Florida 17	Cigar	119
Besuki H382 (Ambulu)	Cigar	103	Florida Sumatra	Cigar	120
Besuki H382 (Kesilir)	Cigar	104	Frog Eye Orinoco	Bright	34
Besuki (Java)	Cigar	105	Galickii	Cigar	121
Big Gem	Bright	23	Glessnor	Cigar	122
Bolivian Criollo Black	Dark	172	Gold Dollar	Bright	35
Bonanza	Bright	24	Gold Leaf 939	Bright	36
Bosikappal	Primitive	259	Gold Leaf Orinoco	Bright	37
Brasil Dunkel	Cigar	106	Golden Burley	Burley	77
Bravyi 200	Unclassified	291	Golden Harvest	Bright	38
Brasilia 7	Rustica	278	Golden Wilt	Bright	39
Brown & Williams Low Nic	Bright	25	Goose Creek Red	Dark	173
Bucak	Bright	26	Goyano	Bright	40
Burley 21	Burley	74	Green Brior	Burley	78
Burley 64	Burley	75	Greenwood	Dark	174
Burley 9	Burley	73	Guácharo	Primitive	264
Bursa	Oriental	209	Habano 2000	Cigar	123
Canik	Oriental	210	Hacienda del Cura	Cigar	124
Catterton	Maryland	189	Harmanli	Oriental	217
Celikhan	Oriental	211	Harmanliiska Basma 163	Oriental	218
Chapeollo	Primitive	260	Harrow Velvet	Burley	79
Cherry Red	Bright	27	Hasenkeyf	Rustica	279
Chichicaste	Primitive	261	Havana 142	Cigar	125
Chillard's White Angel Leaf	Burley	76	Havana 263	Cigar	126
Citir	Oriental	212	Havana 322	Cigar	127
Clevelandii	Wild	289	Havana 38	Cigar	128

Havana 608	Cigar	129	MD A30	Maryland	191
Havana K2	Cigar	130	Meechurinski	Oriental	228
Havana K2-24	Cigar	131	Metacomet	Cigar	145
Havana Z992	Cigar	132	Mohawk	Rustica	282
Helena	Bright	41	Moldovan 456	Burley	86
Herzegovina Flor	Oriental	219	Mont-Calme Brun (Brown)	Cigar	146
Hickory Pryor	Bright	42	Monte Calme Yellow	Burley	87
Hyang Cho	Primitive	265	Moonlight	Cigar	147
Incekara	Oriental	220	Mopan Mayan	Primitive	268
India Black	Dark	175	Mostrenco	Primitive	269
Isleta Pueblo	Rustica	280	Mountain Pima	Primitive	270
Izmir (Lebanon)	Oriental	223	Mutki	Oriental	229
Izmir Ozbas	Oriental	222	Nacional	Cigar	148
Izmir-Karabaglar	Oriental	221	Native 10 (Bolivia)	Cigar	149
Iztepeque	Primitive	266	Native 9 (Bolivia)	Oriental	230
Jaffna	Bright	43	NB-11	Burley	88
Jalapa	Cigar	133	NC 82	Bright	46
Jamaica Wrapper	Cigar	134	Nevrokop 5	Oriental	231
Japan 8	Oriental	224	No. 3666 Deli	Cigar	150
Jasmine	Ornamental	256	Nostrano del Brenta	Cigar	151
Kanburi	Cigar	135	Ohio Dutch	Cigar	152
Karabaglar	Rustica	281	Okinawa	Oriental	271
Keller	Maryland	190	Olor (Dominican Republic)	Cigar	153
Kelly Burley	Burley	80	One Sucker	Dark	179
Krumovgrad 58	Oriental	225	Only the Lonely	Ornamental	257
Kumanovo	Oriental	226	Ostrolist	Bright	47
KY 15	Burley	81	Oxford 207	Bright	48
KY 17	Burley	82	Papante	Primitive	272
KY 190	Burley	83	Paris Wrapper	Bright	49
KY 8635	Burley	84	Pennbel 69	Maryland	194
L'Assomption 201	Cigar	136	Pennsylvania Red	Cigar	154
Lancaster Seed Leaf	Cigar	137	Pergeu	Cigar	155
Lattaquie 92	Oriental	227	Perique	Unclassified	292
Lemon Bright	Bright	44	Piloto Cubano (PR)	Cigar	156
LI Burley 21	Burley	85	Piloto Cubano PR Broad	Cigar	157
Liquiça	Dark	176	Polish	Bright	50
Little Cuba	Primitive	267	Prancak N-1	Oriental	232
Little Dutch	Cigar	138	Pretinho	Primitive	273
Little Yellow	Dark	177	Prilep 66-9/7	Oriental	233
Lizard Tail Orinoco	Bright	45	Prilep 79-94	Oriental	234
Long Red	Cigar	139	Punche	Rustica	283
Machu Picchu Havana	Cigar	140	Punta De Lanza	Cigar	158
Madole	Dark	178	Quadrivalvis	Wild	290
Magnolia	Cigar	141	Reams 158	Bright	51
Manila Wrapper	Cigar	142	Red Rose	Cigar	159
Matsukawa	Cigar	143	Red Russian	Unclassified	293
Matsukawa Kanto 201	Cigar	144	Rejina	Oriental	235
MD 201	Maryland	192	Rot Front	Dark	180
MD 609	Maryland	193	Sacred Cornplanter	Rustica	284
			Sacred Wyandot	Rustica	285

Tobacco Plant Varieties for Home Growers

Samsun	Oriental	236	TN 90 LC	Burley	97
Samsun Maden	Oriental	237	Trabzon	Oriental	245
San Andrés	Cigar	160	Turkish 1	Oriental	246
Shirazi	Oriental	238	Turkish 2	Oriental	247
Shirey	Dark	181	Uruguay	Cigar	164
Shtambur	Rustica	286	Vallejano	Cigar	165
Silk Leaf	Bright	52	Variegata Samsun	Oriental	248
Silver River	Unclassified	294	Vavilov	Oriental	249
Simox	Oriental	239	Vesta 64	Bright	64
Small Stalk Black Mammoth	Dark	182	Viqueque	Dark	187
Smyrna 9	Oriental	240	Virginia 116	Bright	60
Sobolchskii	Burley	89	Virginia 15	Bright	58
Sobolchskii 193	Burley	91	Virginia 24	Bright	59
Sobolchskii 33	Burley	90	Virginia 355	Dark	186
Sorotooskaia	Rustica	287	Virginia 509	Burley	98
Southern Beauty	Bright	53	Virginia 647	Bright	61
Spectrum	Burley	92	Virginia Bright Leaf	Bright	62
Staghorn	Dark	183	Virginia Gold	Bright	63
Stolak 17	Bright	54	Vuelta Abajo	Cigar	166
Suifu	Cigar	161	Walker's Broadleaf	Dark	188
Sultansko	Oriental	241	White Flower (Cuzco)	Oriental	250
Swarr-Hibshman	Cigar	162	White Gold	Bright	65
Sylvestris	Ornamental	258	White Mammoth	Bright	66
Symbol 4	Burley	93	White Stem Orinoco	Bright	67
Szamosi Dark	Dark	184	Wisconsin 901	Cigar	167
Tabaco Colorado	Primitive	274	Wisconsin Seedleaf	Cigar	168
Tabaco Negro (SPAIN)	Dark	185	Xanthi-Yaka 18A	Oriental	251
Tabasqueño Prieto	Primitive	275	Xanthy	Oriental	252
Tasova	Oriental	242	Yayladag	Oriental	253
Tekkekoy	Oriental	243	Yellow 109	Rustica	288
Tekne	Oriental	244	Yellow Gold	Bright	68
Ternopolski 7	Bright	55	Yellow Leaf	Bright	69
Ternopolski 14	Bright	56	Yellow Orinoco	Bright	70
Thailand	Bright	57	Yellow Pryor	Bright	71
Thompson	Maryland	195	Yellow Twist Bud	Burley	99
Timor	Cigar	163	Yenidje	Oriental	254
TN 86	Burley	94	Yumbo	Primitive	276
TN 86 LC	Burley	95	Zimmer Spanish	Cigar	169
TN 90	Burley	96			

END

www.ingramcontent.com/pod-product-compliance
Lightning Source LLC
Chambersburg PA
CBHW060509300426
44112CB00017B/2598